DATE DUE

American Broadcast Regulation
and the First Amendment

American Broadcast Regulation and the First Amendment

Another Look

Charles H. Tillinghast

Iowa State University Press / Ames

For Mary

CHARLES TILLINGHAST practiced corporate and business law in California for over thirty years. Much of his practice involved the recording industry. Upon retirement from practice, Mr. Tillinghast moved to Arizona where he taught media law with an emphasis on the Communications Act of 1932 and the FCC for five years in the Media Arts Department of the University of Arizona.

Iowa State University Press
2121 South State Avenue, Ames, Iowa 50014

Orders: 1-800-862-6657
Office: 1-515-292-0140
Fax: 1-515-292-3348
Web site: www.isupress.edu

♾ Printed on acid-free paper in the United States of America

First edition, 2000

Library of Congress Cataloging-in-Publication Data

Tillinghast, Charles H.
   American broadcast regulation and the First Amendment: another look / by Charles H. Tillinghast—1st ed.
      p. cm.
   Includes bibliographical references and index.
   ISBN 0-8138-2568-7 (alk. paper)
      1. Broadcasting—Law and legislation—United States. 2. Freedom of the press—United States. I. Title.

KF2805.T55 2000
343.7309'94—dc21   00-024682

The last digit is the print number: 9 8 7 6 5 4 3 2 1

Contents

Foreword

We enter the new century in the midst of an unprecedented concentration in the number of giant corporations that rule the U.S. and global mass media. From the mid 1980s to the present, a tidal wave of mergers and acquisitions in the media industries has left eight or nine giants ruling the roost, with the four largest media firms being Time Warner, Disney, Viacom and Rupert Murdoch's beloved News Corporation. What is striking about this concentration is that these firms are now media conglomerates, meaning that they are dominant players in numerous distinct media sectors. Indeed, the notion that a firm can "merely" make films, or music, or publish books, or run a broadcast network is dead. The economics of the media industry make it virtually impossible for small firms or firms that operate in only one field to compete in the long run; hence, they no longer exist.

Among these nine media giants one finds the owners of all the major Hollywood film studios, all but one of the five music companies that sell nearly 90 percent of U.S. music, a majority of U.S. book publishers, and the sole or partial owners of virtually every commercially viable cable television channel. And, of course, there is television. These giants own all six of the U.S. television networks and the vast majority of the major commercial television stations in the 15 or 20 largest markets. With recently announced plans by the Federal Communications Commission to deregulate TV station ownership restrictions further, we can expect the media giants to gobble up hundreds of more stations in the coming months and years.

As Mr. Tillinghast observes, regardless of the conduct of these companies, this amount of media power being consolidated into so few hands is immediately troubling if one holds to any known theory of liberal democracy. When one also factors in the extreme wealth of the largest shareholders and the privileges of the managers, as well as the incessant turn to commercialism to maximize shareholder return, the U.S. media system appears deeply flawed.

It is also absurd. The giants do not exist because of talented entrepreneurs riding to victory in the free and competitive market, slaying their competitors with better products at lower prices. These giants exist as they do, and with as much power as they enjoy, not because of the workings of the free market, but due to the workings of the government. It was the government that allocated extremely valuable broadcast licenses (giving semimonopolistic power) to these firms and received not one penny in return for them. This has been an example of corporate welfare that dwarfs all the government "handouts" to poor people—much criticized in the commercial media and mainstream political culture—by a factor of at least 10 and maybe as large as 100 or more.

The theoretical justification for this world-class graft is that the FCC made public service requirements on the fortunate few commercial broadcasters who got (would it be unfair to say "stole" if we wish to use the language most accurately?) the highly desired broadcast licenses. Public service broadcasting meant, in theory, that commercial broadcasters would do programming that they would not do otherwise if their sole purpose was to maximize profit. The entire history of U.S. broadcast regulation has been one of ineffectual and toothless regulation producing precious little public service. In comparison to the rugged regulation of commercial broadcasters in Britain from the 1950s to the 1980s—where the commercial stations were often close to the BBC in public service output—the U.S. regulation produced pathetic, laughable results.

There were a handful of solid regulations that were put in place, mostly because they did not take money immediately out of the pockets of the commercial broadcasters. These included stipulations against one firm owning more than a handful of stations, rules preventing TV networks from producing their own entertainment programs, the Equal Time rule, and the Fairness Doctrine. A main impetus to the wave of consolidation among media firms in the 1990s was the relaxation or elimination of many of the restrictions on broadcasting and media ownership. It opened the floodgates to concentrated ownership. Indeed, were the ownership rules maintained where they were 20 years ago, the current media system would have been unthinkable. In sum, the corporate media system is the direct result of government subsidies and policies.

But what is most striking about these government subsidies and policies is how they have been made with virtually no public input whatsoever. The seminal 1996 Telecommunications Act, which Tillinghast discusses herein, was written by and for big business with zero public involvement. Two factors explain this state of affairs. First, there is almost no coverage of these issues in the news, except in the business and trade press, where coverage is directed to investors and managers, not citizens. Second, as with most other political issues in the United States, the range of debate is determined by where the money is. Because there are no powerful monied special interests fighting against the existing commercial broadcasting and media regime, the boundaries of legitimate debate are set by the battles between the huge corporate lobbies over who can get the biggest slice of the pie. But that the corporations automatically get the pie is a given, and not subject to any questioning in mainstream political circles.

A crucial aspect of this increasing corporate domination of the broadcasting and media system has been the compliance of some in the academic community. Sometimes this compliance has assumed the form of outright advocacy on behalf of corporate media interests, dressed up in the freechoice rhetoric of Chicago School economic theory. Charles Tillinghast has done a very good job in this book of carefully dismantling the arguments of the legal wing of this probusiness juggernaut. Indeed, when one looks closely at the work of Hayek, Friedman and other free market worshippers, it becomes clear that their work has a thinly disguised contempt for democracy, as that might permit the public to interfere with business domination of society. Hence the modern-day free market advocates have no qualms about increasing the dominance of corporations in the name of democracy, because in their Orwellian world corporate domination, hypercommercialism and public powerlessness is the acme of the good society, a.k.a. democracy.

But the most important case for deregulating broadcasters (except, of course, to have the government protect the firms' monopoly control over their frequencies from so-called "pirates") is invariably wrapped in the First Amendment. No government intervention into their affairs! This is a brilliant tactical move for the corporate media—as it is for the tobacco industry, advertisers and other charlatans—as the First Amendment provides a sacred fig leaf to mask their naked self-interest. And the First Amendment has appeal across the political spectrum, so these claims appeal even to those highly skeptical about corporations and business domination of social life.

In this book Charles Tillinghast has done an admirable job of clarifying the relationship of the First Amendment to broadcasting. He has also made a powerful case on behalf of genuine regulation of broadcasting in the public interest. If the United States is ever to begin to approach anything remotely near a genuine participatory democracy, it will require a broadcasting and media system set up to serve Main Street (and all other streets) as much as Wall Street and Madison Avenue. That is why the battle for media reform is a cornerstone for all social movements wishing to reverse the astonishing growth of social inequality and depoliticization in the United States in the past generation. And in this democratic struggle, Charles Tillinghast's book will provide a valuable corrective to corporate propaganda.

Robert W. McChesney
University of Illinois

Preface

Following a law practice of over 30 years, I was fortunate to teach an undergraduate survey course at the University of Arizona dealing with legal aspects of media regulation, a course largely devoted to broadcasting as regulated under the Communications Act. Naturally enough, I was exposed to detailed consideration of the contentions of various libertarian voices urging an end of government regulation of the broadcast medium. The basis for their deregulatory arguments consisted in large measure of criticism, often to the point of ridicule, of reasoning by the Supreme Court in two of its major broadcast law decisions, *NBC v. U.S.* and *Red Lion Broadcasting Company, Inc. v. FCC.* I found something about these arguments unsettling.

The written opinions in the two cases are complex and often difficult to decipher. What exactly was the Court saying? I decided to read the briefs filed by the parties and concluded that crediting the cases with decisions they are usually believed to have announced was in error. As a consequence, validity of the criticisms leveled at those decisions was undercut because they were aimed at "straw men," that is, at decisions the court had not made. This discovery provided one purpose for writing this book.

A second purpose rose in part from my talking to radio engineers about nonlegal aspects of radio operations as they might bear on legal matters. Communication was often difficult. Due to engineering ignorance, I sometimes failed to ask the right questions, or at least in the right way, while the engineers' immersion in their field and lack of legal training sometimes led them to misinterpret my questions, producing answers that confused me. This experience was part of a larger one arising from the fact that there was no one with legal training with whom I could talk about my concerns. There are virtually no lawyers outside of Washington, D.C., who know much about the Communications Act and FCC operations. Partly a result of an early FCC decision to conduct its activities exclusively in the nation's capital, it is also a consequence of the fact, noted by Michigan Law

School dean Lee Bollinger in his book *Images of a Free Press*, that no law school in the country devotes much, if any, course content to the legal side of broadcasting. That issues involving one of our most important national educational forces are neglected in our law schools is not merely "unfortunate"; it is the likely cause of a general failure of legal professionals to bring their expertise to bear on policy issues relative to broadcasting and the larger field of "telecommunications" under which broadcasting is increasingly subsumed. Aside from law review articles, usually concerned with particular court cases, the major policy work in this field has been done almost exclusively by nonlawyer academics, primarily from the fields of journalism and communications. This book is a modest attempt to lessen the imbalance.

Because I had few people with whom to discuss my thoughts and the contents of this book, it is obvious that its errors are mine. I owe a debt of gratitude to my wife, who ungrudgingly read draft after draft to help me avoid my greatest sin, wordiness. The credit is hers to the extent I succeeded. Others read separate chapters, and their comments were of great value. I refrain from naming them solely to avoid imputing to them any responsibility greater than they assumed.

Introduction

When the *Titanic* was sinking in 1912 and Marconi wireless
equipment was used to send distress signals out into the ether,
the signals were often garbled by interference from other transmitters. Receiving help would have required signals from the *Titanic* giving her position clearly. As we know, timely help was not received: In the
absence of some miracle, such help could not possibly have reached the
ship without signal clarity. No one could have known where to find her.

Before the wireless, messages could be sent around the world only by
means of cable, which required land-based stations. When wireless became
available, ships at sea like the *Titanic*, which had been unable to use cable,
at last had a means of rapid communication. However, signal interference
was characteristic of the ether through which wireless transmissions were
carried. Interference presented a serious obstacle to reliable use of wireless,
at sea or otherwise. Navies, while making use of the technology, were also
concerned about this problem. The mightiest navy in the world at that
time, the British, quickly adopted Marconi equipment. The U.S. Navy also
wanted to make use of that technology, but British Marconi, its owner, attached conditions the Americans found unacceptable. For neither navy, of
course, would use of the equipment have been free of the signal interference problem.

In 1912 Congress decided that requirement of a license for those
wishing to transmit through the ether in the United States appeared to afford a method for some control over the interference problem. It was
known that Morse code signals (the "language" of transmission then in
use) could be restricted to specific frequencies, or portions of the ether, as
defined by wavelengths. If persons sending such Morse code messages into
the air were licensed, and thereby restricted to use of certain frequencies,
at a certain power and from a specified location, at least the source of interference could be detected. Thus did licensing become part of the 1912
Radio Act, and licensing has marched hand in hand with broadcasting ever

since, becoming the principal thread in the warp and woof of American broadcasting today.

In 1912 broadcasting as we now know it—sound and pictures coming out of a box, day in and day out, on many channels from which we can select different programs, all scheduled in advance for our convenience— was, it seems safe to say, anticipated by no one. Use of wireless for broadcasting has wrought many changes, but its use continues to be subject to licensing: One may not broadcast without a license from the federal government. Most broadcasters probably wish licensing could be dispensed with, but because it was and is the means by which signal interference is prevented; broadcasters can't seem to do without it[1].

The broadcaster depends on having available a clear channel on which to communicate with his audience so that he can sell that audience to advertisers who choose his station to push sale of their products. The government, as licensor, polices the spectrum, preventing signal interference with broadcasters' transmissions, assuring them of the monopoly status over their frequencies they require to meet their advertisers' needs.

The licensing system also provided government with an opening to exercise influence over program content, and Congress took the opening by imposing on licensees certain obligations to serve the public interest. Over time broadcasters have become more and more unhappy with efforts by the government to enforce this public service requirement. However, when presented with opportunities to attack the validity of their status as government licensees, broadcasters have proved timid, apparently fearing that the whole edifice of the Communications Act might be brought down if they were too bold, leaving them once again with the signal interference from which licensing protected them.

Failure of broadcasters to seek decisive judicial relief from government regulation has not left them totally without remedy. They attempted to minimize government interference with their activities by trying to control FCC decision making. They also sought to persuade all who would listen, the Supreme Court included, that the government's role should be limited to prevention of signal interference.

In the two best-known cases in which broadcasters could have litigated the constitutionality of licensing, *NBC v. U.S.* and *Red Lion Broadcasting Company, Inc. v. FCC*, the Court in its written opinions described the spectrum as involving scarcity, a factual condition referred to by the justices as the reason why government licensing is necessary. Some students of broadcast law have read such statements by the Court as "holdings" that licensing does not offend the Constitution, specifically the First Amendment. However, these assertions by the Court are not sufficiently free of ambiguity to render such a conclusion incontestable. They can just as easily be read as simply restatements by the Court in summary form of the positions of the parties as understood by the Court. Support for reading them this way can be found in the fact that no party in either of these cases contended licensing was unconstitutional. The Supreme Court traditionally refrains from deciding constitutional questions unless it finds itself compelled to do so. It is not apparent that the Court was under any such compulsion in either of those cases. That those statements are not meaningless in the context of reading these decisions as dealing with questions other than the constitutionality of the broadcasters' status as a government licensee adds weight to the conclusion that in fact the two cases did not purport to decide that issue.

However, critics of government regulation of broadcasting (often academics) have utilized statements made in the Court's decisions as platforms from which to attack any government regulation of broadcasting beyond that needed to prevent signal interference. Arguing that the Court made these statements in support of conclusions to validate the Communications Act in the face of a First Amendment infringement claim, such critics find the logic and factual assertions contained in them to be of dubious validity. Such analyses have been widely publicized and have had the effect of casting doubt on the intellectual bona fides of those two Supreme Court decisions. Although many have disagreed with the deregulatory outlook of such critics, no one has contended, as this book does, that the force of the critics' arguments against the Court's reasoning is dependent on a misreading of the opinion in each case.

Apart from misunderstanding the two Supreme Court decisions, some critics claim broadcasters should be entitled to all the First Amendment rights the Constitution bestows on print media, regardless of the *NBC* and *Red Lion* decisions. While acknowledging that it is unlikely that the Supreme Court will change the current law under which the First Amendment rights of broadcasters have been held inferior to those of the press, these critics urge that nonetheless, as a matter of public policy, broadcasters should be "entitled" to the same First Amendment rights as the press because the function of broadcasters is indistinguishable from that of the press. Like the press, broadcasters should be free of government pressure to "serve the public interest." This contention fails to take account of the effect on broadcast journalism of the licensee-status of FCC licensees, which effect I contend works against the proposed policy. Collectively, the arguments of the critics have resulted in a steady decline in assertion of FCC regulatory power over broadcast content.

Two interweaving threads, then, have worked to shape today's broadcasting, both centered on the fact of licensing. The first is the question of the meaning of the constitutional guarantee of freedom of speech/press relative to broadcasting. The second derives from arguments that opponents of government regulation of broadcasting base upon two Supreme Court opinions as they interpret them. To these now must be added a third, seemingly unrelated string—the fact of the dominant position of corporations in the broadcast medium. That, in turn, requires preliminary consideration of some aspects of modern economic theory.

Most opponents of government regulation of broadcasting are of a certain Libertarian persuasion, usually associated with teachings of the Chicago school of economics. Adherents to that school, which seems to influence most economic thinking today, put their faith in the functioning of free markets as a sort of panacea to all societal problems. The Chicago school believes that markets, defined by free choices of buyers and sellers, acting rationally in their own interest, and fully informed, will provide optimum use and allocation of all economic resources. Disregarding questions like the meaning of "free" relative to choice, what qualifies a consumer as being "fully informed," and whether consumer decisions are generally rational (or intended by "informational" advertising so to be), they believe the most serious interference with optimal realization of such markets comes from government. Government intrusion in market operation is a disservice, substituting bureaucratic or legislative determinations of how such resources should be allocated in place of the automatic allocation decided by the "invisible hand" of the price mechanism.

The roots of Chicago school thought can be traced back in history to many sources, but to do so is not my purpose. It is enough to be aware that in its contemporary form, naturally attracted by the individual freedom celebrated in its goals, it finds its primary justification in its theoretical claim to allocate economic resources (all "scarce") at minimal cost. When evaluating claims of the Chicago school relative to broadcasting, at least, one must consider the nature of corporations, the format through which most American business is conducted.

Use of the corporate structure is not new. It has been the organizational form of choice for conducting business in the United States, including broadcasting, starting at least as far back as the 1870s. Today anyone may form a corporation under state statutes. It was not always so easy; before the Civil War grant of a charter to operate as a corporation was a prerogative of government, not necessarily easily obtained. Such charters were usually granted by states for the purpose of accomplishing some public objective. As American business looked more and more to use of the corporate form, and states increasingly had less need to use corporations for particular public purposes, state legislatures yielded to the importuning of wealthy businessmen and greatly relaxed regulatory aspects of their corporation laws. American business became increasingly interstate, rendering largely ineffective even the amount of state regulation that survived business pressures. States were led to become suitors of prospective incorporations rather than regulators, so desirous were they of the franchise tax revenues that would come from incorporation of a successful business in that state.

With the growth of giant corporations in the last quarter of the 19th century, both in manufacturing and banking, public pressure led to enactment of antitrust laws intended to curb monopolistic tendencies and the resulting evils. After the initial burst of such antitrust legislation, the American public seemed satisfied, and there has been little action by Congress in this field since. The numbers of truly immense corporations has grown; their control over wide aspects of the American economy has expanded.

The information distribution systems of this country have been affected by these developments much as any other sector of business enterprise. But broadcasting is not just another business. It is of vital importance in the dissemination of information, knowledge of which is of great importance for an informed citizenry. Broadcasting is uniquely pervasive of the American home. Primarily a source of entertainment, it also supplies news and political analysis. It is in the performance of the latter functions that more than 90 percent of the American electorate say they rely on broadcasting as the source of most of their information about the world. It is that fact which provides the best evidence of the medium's "uniquely pervasive" position in American homes, and it is that fact which should make us aware of the awesome power of broadcasting to mold public opinion. In light of the unique nature of broadcasting, the quality of "corporateness" takes on a significance it might lack in other areas of modern life. The number of corporations in broadcasting has shrunk while the survivors have increased in both size and power. Simultaneously, the corporation has evolved in a manner that increases the danger to a democratic society from corporate dominance of broadcasting. The corporations that now control this powerful medium cannot be depended upon, unaided, to provide the American public with the full information necessary for informed self-government. Such entities are often involved in other business activities that may be unrelated to broadcasting and may be more important as revenue generators than are their broadcasting interests; and they must always give priority to serving the investment interests of their shareholder-owners. Consequently, such corporations are not set up, in law or in fact, to perform the educational function of keeping the American peo-

ple informed. The FCC once sought to limit ownership of broadcast outlets. Supplementing that policy, designed to maximize the exercise of independent editorial judgments in the medium, the government also imposed on broadcasters an affirmative duty to provide coverage of
controversial issues. Known as the "fairness doctrine," this policy was abandoned in 1987, action that testified to the triumph of Chicago school
thinking in the broadcast regulatory arena.

In 1996 many of the corporations involved in the electromagnetic
spectrum acted, with congressional approval, as authors of the Telecommunications Act. The full impact of that legislation remains uncertain,
though it seems clearly to have eviscerated much broadcaster accountabil-
ity to the public and to have undercut government power to require broadcasting to serve the public interest. It certainly sharply curtailed FCC efforts to limit the number of broadcast stations that could be under
common ownership.

I believe the fairness doctrine, or something much like it, should be
resurrected, and this book is intended to make a case for such resurrection.
I address the arguments of critics of government regulation of broadcasting, whether aimed at the presumed Supreme Court jurisprudence already
mentioned, or stated independently of such jurisprudence. I also argue
that broadcasters cannot escape their status as licensees of the government
and that such status, as well as the nature of the medium itself, provides
strong support for regulation of use of the electromagnetic spectrum.

My argument is presented in the context of an exploration of the
paths by which we have reached our current state of affairs. Although I do
not present an exhaustive history, I believe this book provides sufficient detail to give an accurate picture of the means by which broadcasting, as regulated by government, took the shape it now has. My hope is that average
citizens with above average curiosity concerning the influence of broadcasting on their lives will find some new understanding of broadcasting as
it exists today. The book should also bring into sharper focus the possibilities and the dangers broadcasting presents for the future. And of course I
hope that publication of this work may lead to, or at least contribute to,
restoration of the fairness doctrine.

Notes

1. Some alternatives to licensing have been suggested but not tested. See
Coase 1959, 1, and DeVany et al. 1980.

American Broadcast Regulation and the First Amendment

CHAPTER 1

Origins of Broadcasting:
Three Inventors and a Seer

Although many persons contributed to the development of broadcasting, four individuals stand out for purposes of this book. Three of them, Guglielmo Marconi, Lee De Forest, and Howard Armstrong, were inventors. The fourth, David Sarnoff, was a businessman. American patent law and the United States Navy also played significant parts in the story of early radio, and those parts, too, are explored in this chapter along with these four individuals.

Guglielmo Marconi

Building on earlier inventions, broadcasting may be said to have been "born" in the last decades of the 19th century. Guglielmo Marconi conceived a means for transmission of signals through the air, which could be made comprehensible by use of Morse code. With encouragement from the British government and navy, Marconi's achievement was exploited by British commercial interests. Young American inventors improved on Marconi's work, but patent law, designed to encourage inventions by giving inventors exclusive exploitation rights, operated in this highly technical field instead to frustrate the inventor's reward, leaving exploitation of the wireless in the hands of corporations, which had the means to gain control of wireless art through patent acquisition. Individual inventors were gradually eliminated from the field of wireless communication, leaving its development to corporate entrepreneurs with the vision and means to exploit its uses.

Experiments conducted in the last quarter of the 19th century by a young German, Heinrich Hertz (whose name was applied to the measurement of radio frequencies), provided the incentive for Marconi's efforts. Hertz had succeeded in transmitting electromagnetic impulses through the air to be captured by his "receiver" as sparks. But it was Marconi whose work turned the new forces released by Hertz into technology that could be made usable in practical ways.

Scion of a wealthy Italian and his Anglo-Irish wife, Marconi pursued the mysteries unlocked by Hertz. Marconi's father thought him something of a lunatic, but his mother, like almost all mothers, thought him the last word in all things smart and wonderful. He *was* smart. He succeeded in improving upon Hertz's work by adapting for his transmitter a telegraph key originally designed for sending Morse-code transmissions via wire, and using as his receiver a "coherer," a glass tube with wires protruding at each end, which activated electrical impulses when metal filings inside the tube were magnetized. By use of these devices Marconi was able to transmit and receive Hertz-like electronic impulses over considerable distances and varied terrain. The coherer carried the impulses to a "moving pen," which recorded the Morse-code dots and dashes on rotating graph paper, as was done in telegraphy by means of wire.

Failing to interest the Italian government in his invention—whether because of its lack of vision or doubts based on Marconi's youth—Marconi turned toward England, where his mother's influential friends offered some entrée into upper government circles. The suspicious-looking equipment he was carrying en route almost kept him out of England, but, obstacles cleared, he finally got a hearing. British authorities liked what they saw and encouraged Marconi to establish a wireless communications network around the world, or at least so much of it as interested the British. A good deal of it did.

Marconi and his backers established the Marconi Wireless Telegraph Company in England and a Marconi subsidiary in the United States, the Marconi Wireless Company of America (American Marconi). The main function of the latter was to hold the few working assets used in stations in the United States where Marconi equipment was located. It was also party to patent licensing agreements with its British parent, covering the Marconi technology. These patents were foundational for the corporations' operating technology. As it turned out, failure to look beyond that technology brought the corporations' business to an end.

The modus operandi of British Marconi was to set up transmitters and receivers at a sufficient number of land stations to permit communication with as many ship locations as possible, given the limited reach of the wireless telegraphy signals. Because British Marconi controlled the patent rights, ships wishing to have such wireless communication capability had to deal with that corporation. The corporate policy of British Marconi required that it retain ownership of the wireless equipment on board the vessel involved; that the user agree to communicate only with Marconi receiving equipment; and that the operator on the vessel be a Marconi employee.

In 1904 an English engineer on Marconi's payroll, John Fleming, created the diode vacuum tube. This tube performed most of the functions of Marconi's coherer and became the foundation for most of the later inventions in the development of radio, starting with the audion (triode vacuum tube) created by Lee De Forest. Though English Marconi had patented the Fleming diode, the corporation was apparently satisfied with the communication system it had and continued using the coherer, permitting the art of Fleming's diode to languish.

Lee De Forest

Lee De Forest was born in 1873 in Council Bluffs, Iowa. His father was a Congregational minister, and the young De Forest grew up in the surroundings of his father's ministry. In Lee's sixth year his father undertook to educate freed slaves. For this purpose the elder De Forest became president of Talladega College in Alabama some forty miles from Birmingham. Although denominated a college, it was an educational institution at many levels, none anywhere near "collegiate" as we define the term today. The educational needs and diverse capabilities of the freed slaves were numerous, though their preparation in terms of prior education and even familiarity with the nature of education was almost totally lacking. The "college" was in fact more like elementary and secondary schools combined.

The young De Forest grew up at Talladega, where he and his siblings were shunned by the blacks and hated by the local whites, who saw them as elements of the "yankee" enemy. Isolated except from his family, Lee kept himself busy by reading all the scientific journals he could lay his hands on. He developed intense curiosity with respect to the field of electromagnetic waves and use of the "ether," as the medium transporting such waves was then called, for their transmission. He was determined to be an inventor and accomplish great things that would make him famous and wealthy.

Upon completion of his primary education, De Forest entered Mount Hermon, a secondary school run on authoritarian lines, designed to turn out devout young Christians. After Mount Hermon he wanted to go to Yale's new Sheffield Scientific School. Although the school offered a three-year college-level curriculum, it did not provide a "liberal" education, leading Lee's father to oppose the young man's wishes. In the end, however, the elder De Forest relented. An industrious and dedicated student, Lee stayed on at Yale three years beyond the first three, earning his Ph.D.

In 1900 De Forest claimed to have invented a device called the "responder." It performed the function of Marconi's coherer while allowing an operator to use sensitive earphones for receiving signals rather than depending on the ink transcribing devices then in use with the Marconi equipment. De Forest joined forces with a promoter, Abraham White, who set up a corporation to exploit Lee's invention.

Upon hearing of De Forest's claim, a young Canadian inventor, Reginald Aubrey Fessenden, sued De Forest and the corporation alleging that De Forest had stolen the idea for the responder from work Lee had observed in Fessenden's laboratories. While the suit progressed, Abraham White proceeded on his path to sell stock in the De Forest corporation by means both fair and foul, though mostly foul. He did not hesitate to "oversell" the capabilities of the De Forest invention and was later found liable for fraud in connection with these stock sales. De Forest was personally sued along with the corporation and White, but he escaped being found culpable for fraud, as no misrepresentations were traced to him and he had not profited from the stock sales.

Meanwhile, Fessenden's suit proceeded to judgment in his favor, and De Forest lost the responder. The judgment also included an award of money damages against both De Forest and the corporation. The monetary award was predicated on actual damages, because there was no finding that De Forest had acted fraudulently. Nonetheless, De Forest was embittered by the outcome. He believed himself to have been cheated of his rights in the responder and that his good name had been tarnished. Fortunately for De Forest, White found sufficient corporate funds to discharge the money judgment, freeing the impecunious De Forest at least from that worry.

As a final indignity White forced De Forest out of the corporation that bore his name. This actually benefited De Forest in the long run, as the corporation headed for even more trouble. Besides, even though he was short of money, De Forest was able to leave the corporation possessed of his most recent invention on which the corporation had no claim—a "triode" vacuum tube, which De Forest called the "audion." The audion, or triode, marked a significant advance over the diode tube as invented by Fleming.

In the course of his research involving Fleming's diode, De Forest, in what can only be described as a flash of genius, decided to add a small wire to the inside base of the tube. The addition of that wire, creased accordion fashion, produced much stronger signals than did the diode without the wire. Previously faint transmissions lost to the ear were now audible, and the range at which signals could be received was significantly extended. Several times De Forest indicated he didn't understand why the grid he added had the effect it did. Nonetheless, it worked; the mystery of how was ultimately solved by Howard Armstrong.

Edwin Howard Armstrong

Born in New York in 1891, Howard Armstrong moved with his family in 1906 to a commodious home in Yonkers, which was to remain his parental abode until the death of his widowed mother in 1936. At the Yonkers home Armstrong at an early age became an avid student of electromagnetic waves and the possibilities of wireless transmissions.

Armstrong attended the Columbia University School of Mines, Engineering, and Chemistry and while there came to believe that he often had greater knowledge in the spheres of his study than did his instructors. Always careful about detail, and possessed of enormous self-discipline, Armstrong never permitted any unexplained phenomenon in his experiments or the work of others to slip by him until he was able to understand what was happening. His instructors at Columbia often seemed less thorough and demanding than he, and he considered many of them inferior to himself. Armstrong's attitude probably struck some as supercilious. Others considered him a smart aleck. Whatever the reason, Armstrong produced a negative reaction in some faculty members, who opposed letting him graduate. Fortunately, the young man had among his instructors sufficient defenders who recognized his abilities, and he successfully completed his degree program. After graduation he turned his attention to the study of De Forest's audion and the reasons it worked as it did.

Failure to understand how the audion worked led, in its manufacture, to problems of quality control with the result that some of the finished tubes worked better than others. As they were manufactured, they were tested, then graded and priced according to test results. Although purchasers were usually aware that they were or were not getting tubes of top performance, there was still unhappiness among buyers that they had to take what they got.

Though operation of the audion increased the number of signals received as well as their fidelity compared to the Marconi equipment, such signals continued to be electromagnetic pulsations decipherable only in Morse code. Engineers specializing in wireless recognized that, although the audion advanced the prospects for transmission of the human voice, realizing that feat would require the generation of an enormous amount of electrical power. De Forest's old nemesis, Reginald Fessenden, had an idea in mind that might do the trick: an alternator generating power at the rate of 100,000 cycles per second. He turned to experts at General Electric Corporation, where a GE engineer, Ernst Alexanderson, working with Fessenden, succeeded in producing such a device. Although it was named the "Alexanderson alternator" in honor of its principal inventor, the fact that Alexanderson was a GE employee meant that GE was the legal owner of the invention.

Fessenden positioned one of these alternators at Brant Rock, Massachusetts, and on Christmas Eve of 1906 launched a special program into the "ether." Ships and amateurs with receiving equipment within range heard through their headsets a woman's voice singing and Fessenden playing his violin, the first such transmissions known.

Although the Alexanderson alternator performed as anticipated, it was large and expensive, not suitable for use by most. Armstrong, meanwhile, pursued other avenues in attempting to understand how De Forest's audion worked. His research led him to realize that the tube's behavior was a result of the fact that it was conducting electrons. Finding that the current from the plate to the headphones oscillated, Armstrong thought to feed the current back through the grid repeatedly. The result was astounding. It amplified the transmitted sounds, making them steadily louder and finally audible to the human ear without need of headphones. As the audion approached maximum amplification, Armstrong detected a curious hissing noise. Characteristic of the audion, as it turned out, this effect was later found to enable that tube to be used to transmit radio signals as well as to receive them. The Alexanderson alternator could be replaced by the audion, making transmission much easier as well as much less expensive. For the moment, though, the GE-owned Alexanderson alternator was the only reliable transmitter available—Marconi's more limited wireless telegraph excepted—and the only transmitter that carried the human voice.

The first of Armstrong's discoveries, the repeated feeding of the signal back through the tube, was identified as "regeneration"; the second, that is, the use of the tube for transmission purposes, was labeled its "oscillation" feature. In 1913 Armstrong made changes in the audion tube to cause it to emit continuous waves. Though he had developed the regeneration principle in 1911 and the oscillating-transmission feature in 1912, it was not until 1913 that he applied for patents covering both characteristics, a chronology that added complications favorable to De Forest in the later patent litigation between him and Armstrong.

Battle of the Inventors

The audion, enhanced by the regeneration and oscillation features Armstrong discovered in 1911 and 1912, proved central to the operation of radio. Because of lack of funds, combined with the naive belief that his word could not be doubted, Armstrong did not apply for patents on his inventions until late 1913. Over four years later De Forest began what is called an "interference" proceeding in the Patent Office, alleging that Armstrong's patent applications conflicted with his audion patent. This was the initial step in the dispute between the two as to which had been first in discovering these two important audion qualities. The legal battle continued, on and off, for thirty years with increasing hard feelings, and at great financial cost to both. After a determination by the Patent Office in Armstrong's favor, and a decision by federal courts in New York, also in Armstrong's favor, De Forest prevailed in the end. His victory gave him little, as he had in 1915 sold his patent rights in the audion to AT&T for $50,000. For Armstrong, who sold his patent claims to Westinghouse in 1920, the defeat was devastating and bitter.

This litigation between De Forest and Armstrong was only one of a number of patent disputes that retarded radio's development. In 1916 the Marconi Corporation sued De Forest, alleging that De Forest's addition of the wire grid to the Fleming tube constituted only a minor modification of the Fleming diode. Judgment went against De Forest, and he was enjoined from exploiting the audion tube without the consent of Marconi. In a pending suit of his own against American Marconi, De Forest contended that Marconi was unlawfully employing his grid in its tubes without his consent. The Marconi interests settled that case by agreeing not to use the De Forest grid in the Fleming diode without De Forest's permission. Marconi's court victory and the settlement in De Forest's suit left use of the audion in limbo, usable by no one without the consent of both litigants—in short, a stalemate.

Patents

In section 8 of article 1 of the United States Constitution, Congress is empowered to grant limited exploitation rights to inventors for the purpose of promoting "the progress of science and the useful arts." Before 1787 inventions had been primarily mechanical in character. Consequently, it is unlikely the drafters of the Constitution contemplated the possibility that an inventor might be unable to exploit a worthwhile invention if he or she had the financial means to do so.

Congress had adopted legislation to provide a means for inventors to acquire the protections the Constitution contemplated. These patent laws created the Patent Office to process applications for patents, and to grant them when the office concluded the application revealed an invention of sufficient novelty. A patent gave the inventor a monopoly to exploit the invention during the patent's life—17 years then, 20 now. After the patent expired, the invention would fall into the public domain, open to exploitation by anyone.

The field of electronics added a new twist to the operation of patent laws. Not only was the field an obscure one understood by few people, it was also one in which seemingly minor alterations in uses of electromagnetism could be of great significance. Advances tended to build on prior art, and the question whether an advance was sufficiently novel to qualify for a patent in its own right could be difficult to answer. Even "experts" in the Patent Office might have conflicting views. In the end judges, usually without expertise in these matters, made the final determinations. Dependent on the parties for education, the mysteries might remain mysterious—and misunderstood by the judges, a state of affairs of which the parties could be unaware until it was revealed by the court's decision.

For the Patent Office, the volume of patent applications in the early 20th century relative to electronics was a flood compared to that experienced in any prior period. In 1910, 270 patents were granted in the field of radio communication; this increased to 350 in 1912, and the pace showed no sign of diminishing.

Patent rights, intended to promote progress in the sciences, in the case of the audion became a roadblock to progress. Conflicting claims between Marconi and De Forest, between Fessenden and De Forest, and between De Forest and Armstrong combined to produce an environment in which risks of liability for patent infringement put a stop to much work in the field. This left the Marconi interests possessed of the only operational system for engaging in wireless communication, ensuring continuance of its monopoly status.

Used as intended, patents could encourage scientific development by rewarding the inventor. But the resulting (and intended) monopolies could also operate to inhibit further research. Patented inventions like Fleming's, owned but neglected by Marconi, errected a barrier to new research, while the patent also prevented use by others of the covered art. Rapid development of means for exploiting use of the electromagnetic spectrum placed patent rights in the hands of a number of individual inventors and some corporations. The impasse that resulted seemed to put a halt to development of radio technology.

David Sarnoff: Seer and Businessman

In 1896, when David Sarnoff was five, his father came to the United States, leaving David and the rest of the family behind in the Russian city of Minsk. As Jews, the Sarnoffs had known the persecution of members of their faith. David's father was a house painter in Russia and could aspire no higher. For his children and himself he hoped for better in the new world. But first he had to get them all there, a goal he attained in 1900 after four years alone in the United States working long hours at low-paying jobs.

Upon their arrival in America, the Sarnoff family found that Sarnoff senior was sicker than when he had left them in 1896. Suffering from consumption and great weakness, he was a skeleton of his former self. The Sarnoffs lived in squalid tenements in New York, David's mother taking in sewing and any other work she could to help keep the family going in face of her husband's physical disabilities.

Soon after arrival in New York from Russia, young David realized that if he did not help his mother sustain the family, no one else would. He sold newspapers, rising each day before dawn to distribute a number of journals to various outlets. He also gradually acquired routes and stands of his own, developing a sense of self-sufficiency and self-discipline before he reached his teens. So began his path to becoming what later was termed a "workaholic." The time he devoted to gainful employment combined with the time he devoted to getting an education seemed to eat up more hours than there were in each day. This early experience of incessant work without relaxation or recreation may have formed the personality of a man who later showed no sign of needing either.

Sarnoff's life came to a crossroad in 1906, the year of Fessenden's famous Christmas Eve transmission of the human voice. Wanting to make more money and having worked with newspapers, Sarnoff went to what he thought were the offices of the *New York Herald* to apply for a job as a reporter. By chance he had actually gone to the site of another business owned by Gordon Bennett, the *Herald*'s publisher. It was the Commercial Cable Company, which was engaged in the business of transmitting messages via Britain's transatlantic cable. He was hired as a messenger boy, but the job lasted only a few months. Following denial of his request for three days off during Rosh Hashanah and Yom Kippur so that he could sing with his synagogue choir during the high holy days, an appeal of the denial led to his being fired. It may have been his first experience with anti-Semitism in the United States.

In Sarnoff's brief time with the Commercial Cable Company, he learned the Morse code and how to operate and maintain wireless transmitters. He thought himself qualified to be a wireless operator and, after being fired, applied for such a job with American Marconi. He was offered a job as an office boy, a job he took. Thus began his association with American Marconi that continued when RCA took over the functions of American Marconi in 1919. Eventually president of RCA, Sarnoff left that company only at his death in 1971.

A legend developed in the early years of the century in relation to the sinking of the *Titanic*. Sarnoff allegedly had been operating a Marconi wireless in the Wanamaker Tower when the *Titanic* struck the iceberg. Origins of the story that Sarnoff stayed at his receiver all night receiving a stream of signals from the stricken ship are unknown, but Sarnoff never did anything to contradict it. It gave him new visibility and fame, even though, according to Carl Dreher, a longtime business associate and close acquaintance, the story was a fabrication (Dreher 1977, 28). Sarnoff did have some contact via wireless with the *Titanic*, but he was neither alone in that regard nor the primary recipient of the ship's transmissions, and he was not up all night. Wanamaker's, a department store, closed regularly at 5 p.m.

A genuine, and probably more remarkable, story about young Sarnoff concerns his famous 1916 memo to Marconi management. Although many saw the possibility of transmitting the human voice, and thus the possibility of entertainment, Sarnoff appears to have been the first to envision the possibility of broadcasting as we know it today: operation of full-time transmitters sending scheduled entertainment programs to a vast audience, each possessed of a radio receiver. In his memo to Marconi management he described his vision in these words: "A radio telephone transmitter having a range of, say, 25 to 50 miles can be installed at a fixed point where the instrumental or vocal music or both are produced . . . all the receivers attuned to the transmitting wave length should be capable of receiving such music. The receiver can be designed in the form of a simple 'Radio Music Box.'" (Dreher 1977, 39)

Sarnoff urged corporate management to enter into this new line of business involving the manufacture and sale of radio receivers, and the production and broadcast of radio programming. Management showed no interest. As in the past, corporate headquarters in London considered its only business to be worldwide wireless telegraphy via Morse code, a business that it monopolized.

The U.S. Navy

The U.S. Navy had a role to play in the development of radio, a role that grew more significant as a result of the Spanish-American War. At the beginning of that war the U.S. Army was quite small. The force that conquered Cuba, consisting of 18,000 men, was made up primarily of volunteers with relatively little military training. The conquest succeeded, say historians, largely because the Spanish, demoralized and unprepared, were also faced with a well-organized rebellion on the part of elements of the Cuban populace. Another major contributor to the American conquest of the island, though, was the United States Navy, ships of which entered Havana Harbor and neutralized the Spanish naval forces.

Unlike an army, any navy of that time required a large investment for ships. Once such craft are built, it is foolish not to take care of them and to see that they are utilized for the purposes for which they were built. As repositories for such valuable assets, navies naturally took on an importance not possessed by ground forces. This was certainly true for the United States.

Toward the end of the 19th century and early in the 20th the largest navy in the world belonged to Britain. When the British sang, "Rule Britannia, Britannia rules the waves," they were not referring to the airwaves, but to trade routes on the seas. The British navy dominated every ocean of commercial significance, ensuring communication between the "Mother Country" and the rest of the world, in major part for the benefit of British commerce. His Majesty's ships enabled the London government to maintain control of the largest and most extensive empire of recent times. Kaiser Wilhelm, a German cousin of Britain's monarch, so envied King George's navy that he initiated a shipbuilding program to match if not eclipse the British fleet, an effort that contributed significantly to the onset of World War I.

For its part, the U.S. Navy not only played an important part in the 1898 seizure of Cuba, it also was credited with conquering the Philippines by defeating the Spanish fleet in Manila harbor in the same war. The kaiser was not alone in his envy of Britain's navy. As a nation bounded by two oceans, the United States, too, aspired to naval power a good deal greater than that it commanded in 1898.

The American navy thus was vitally interested in ship-to-ship as well as ship-to-shore communication capabilities. To this end the navy had negotiated with Marconi long before the First World War but had been thwarted by the policy of the British corporation, which permitted transmission only from and to Marconi-owned equipment. Not even Marconi's willingness to waive its requirement that it be the employer of operators aboard U.S. naval ships made the arrangement palatable to the United States. The navy looked for alternative means of communication, but largely as a consequence of patent disputes, no other complete and reliable system existed. A method identified as the "Poulsen arc transmitter," developed on the West Coast, failed to prove dependable.

In the course of its search for alternatives to Marconi equipment, the navy entered into a venture with AT&T. The telephone company had approached Lee De Forest in 1912 to purchase rights to his audion, mentioning a purchase price of half a million dollars. Expecting to hear further, and desperate for funds, De Forest heard nothing more until an attorney called on him claiming to represent a client who wished to buy the De Forest audion for $50,000. De Forest was suspicious, but the lawyer swore "on his honor as a gentleman" that AT&T was not the client. In desperate straits De Forest agreed to the sale—only later to learn that the purchaser was indeed AT&T.

Ownership of the audion enabled AT&T to try to develop a wireless telephone. This venture interested the navy, which gave AT&T logistical and other support, including permission to set up a transmitter at a naval facility in Arlington, Virginia. In 1915, using De Forest's audion, the phone company successfully made a wireless "phone" call from Arlington, which was received simultaneously in Paris and Pearl Harbor. Press accounts of the achievement made no mention of De Forest as inventor of the most important technology used in making this effort a success, but credited the navy with its support for AT&T's effort. AT&T even changed the name De Forest had given his invention, rechristening the "audion" the "vacuum tube." AT&T's success failed to provide the navy with the communication system it sought, however, and it was not until 1917 and U.S. entry into the great war that the navy's communications problems were solved.

Prior to 1914, then, Marconi dominated the world of wireless communication. It perceived one possible threat to its position in the Alexanderson alternator, and it made an offer to GE for the purpose of eliminating that threat. It offered to purchase from GE about 20 of the alternators for a substantial sum on condition that Marconi's right to use the alternator would be exclusive. Possession of the alternators on these terms would result in great expansion of Marconi's operating capabilities while at the same time strengthening its monopoly position in wireless telegraphy. However, conditions created by the war apparently prevented Marconi from pursuing this approach to GE, an approach it renewed soon after the war's end.

Broadcast Licensing and World War I

Even as technological advances in radio were stymied by patent disputes and the Marconi monopoly, it became increasingly obvious that use of wireless equipment could provide a major tool for minimizing consequences of disasters at sea. Ships caught in storms or otherwise in distress could use the wireless to relay their positions. Although such ability was limited to the range of such signals, the presence of wireless was nonetheless an improvement over its absence.

Reacting to these facts, Congress in 1910 enacted legislation requiring ships under American jurisdiction and ships using U.S. ports to carry wireless equipment with a range of at least 100 miles. Installing such equipment on ships did not, however, ensure that signals from ships in distress would be heard. Such signals could be made unavailing by interference from other signals, a majority of which were produced by amateurs, who constituted most of the users. There was no system for regulating transmission of interfering signals, a problem of great concern to the civilian shipping industry, which found a powerful ally in the United States Navy.

After the *Titanic* sank in the spring of 1912, pressure from shippers and the navy persuaded Congress to consider new legislation regulating signal interference, leading to adoption of a new Radio Act in the fall of that year. It divided the electromagnetic spectrum (as used in the United States) into two parts: one for use by the government, including the military, and the second for public use. Amateur wireless operators were restricted to the least desirable portion of the spectrum, frequencies of 200 meters or less. Any use of the spectrum by private operators, including the amateurs, required a license from the government. Qualifications for such a license were specified in the act, as were regulations designed to control the wireless equipment in operation. The Department of Commerce was charged with administering the act and issuing licenses.

The 1912 act has been largely trivialized by historians, who have treated it as notable mainly for its failure to provide an effective remedy for the chaotic conditions in broadcasting that developed in the 1920s. Virtually ignored is the fact that the legislation introduced into radio law, almost without debate, the notion that government could require anyone wishing to transmit messages over the airwaves be licensed. Wireless transmissions were to be treated as interstate commerce, because the constitutional authority for congressional adoption of the Radio Act was grounded in the commerce clause. No consideration was given to the possibility that some other part of the Constitution, specifically the First Amendment, might be relevant and that use of wireless might also involve "speech." Newspapers, too, are in interstate commerce, but it is difficult to conceive that anyone would find in the commerce clause sufficient government power to require a license to publish one.

There was little debate of the bill in Congress, though more in the House than in the Senate. Representative James Mann of Illinois, questioning the reach of the commerce clause, asked whether it could authorize regulation of a person's shouting across a state line, to which Ernest Roberts, a congressman from Massachusetts and supporter of the bill, replied that it could if such shouting affected interstate commerce (Cong. Rec. 1912). That was as close as anyone in either chamber came to suggesting that a First Amendment issue might lurk in the proposed statute.

Western Union's wire telegraphy business also involved speech, yet some of its business, including rates, was subject to government regulation. This was because Western Union, a common carrier, was also a "public utility." Starting well before the end of the 19th century, public utilities had been subject to more government regulation than business operations, which didn't fall into that category. In the preface to the 1906 edition of his book, *Cases on Public Service Companies,* Bruce Wyman writes: "Free competition, the very basis of the modern social organization, superseded almost completely medieval restrictions, but it has just come to be recognized that the process of free competition fails in some cases to secure the public good, and it has been reluctantly admitted that some control is necessary over such lines of industry as are affected with a public interest" (iii).

At first glance the operations of Western Union—transmission of communications by wire—appear remarkably similar to transmission of like messages by use of wireless transmitters. It would be natural to assume that if the former operations could be regulated, so could the latter. But regulation of Western Union involved limits on its freedom to set user rates as well as to decide what customers it would serve. It had no impact on the physical transmission of messages, much less their content. The licensing requirement for use of wireless, on the other hand, was a limitation on the right to employ this method of communication at all.

In addition to comparing wireless use to that of Western Union, another reason why no consideration might then have been given to problems of "free speech" may be traced to treatment of the First Amendment since its ratification. Between 1791 and enactment of the Radio Act in 1912, First Amendment questions had come to national prominence only twice. In 1798, barely seven years following ratification of the Bill of Rights, Congress passed the Alien and Sedition acts, making it a crime to criticize the president, any member of his cabinet, or Congress falsely . In adopting these acts, Congress was reacting to what it saw as the threat to the national security posed by activities of U.S. supporters of the French Revolution, who were engaged in drumming up support for that revolution and seeking financial aid for the Jacobin government then in power. Such activities were considered a threat to U.S. political stability and interference with the government's conduct of foreign policy, then neutrally pro-British in Britain's war with France. "Evidence" of pro-Jacobin activity was alleged to have been found in many of the nation's journals, where pro-French and anti-British sentiments were viewed by proponents of the legislation as demonstrating French subversion. Insofar as they dealt with speech issues, the Alien and Sedition acts were primarily aimed at newspaper publishers.

Minority elements in Congress charged that the acts violated the First Amendment, a charge the proponents answered with a somewhat complex argument. The legal system in the states, which had also prevailed when they were colonies, was based on English common law. A major scholar of that law, Sir William Blackstone, had, in his *Commentaries on the Common Law of England* (published in the 1760s, before the revolution), stated that "freedom of the press" gave publishers freedom from interference with respect to what they might publish. It did not, said Blackstone, free the publisher from being punished *after* publication if the matter published were unlawful. The Alien and Sedition acts were, the supporters continued, consistent with this Blackstone definition. No one would be restrained with respect to what he published; punishment for sedition followed only as a *consequence* arising from the publisher's choice of what to publish. Those participating in drafting the Bill of Rights, the argument continued, were certainly familiar with Blackstone's *Commentaries*. Because those persons acquiesced to First Amendment wording identical to that in Blackstone's definition, it was reasonable to assume that they intended the words to have the same meaning as had been ascribed to them by Blackstone.

Opponents of the proposed acts countered that, because the courts of the United States applied the common law in any event, there would have been no need to include in the Constitution guarantees concerning speech or press freedom unless those guarantees were intended to be greater than those within the Blackstone definition. Therefore, inclusion of the First Amendment in the Constitution demonstrated an intended meaning more expansive than Blackstone's.

This position may not be as strong as it appears. The common law can be altered by judicial decisions. Perhaps the First Amendment was put in the Constitution to eliminate the possibility of such change by courts. On the other hand, if the purpose had been merely to prevent judicial alteration, one might expect to have found some indication to that effect in records of the period. No such indication is found.

In the end, the Alien and Sedition acts became law, and there were many prosecutions, usually of newspaper publishers. Such defendants were generally fined—sometimes jailed, though incarceration was rare. When faced with the contention that the acts violated the First Amendment, American courts invariably held them to be valid, citing Blackstone as authority. None of these cases was ever brought to the Supreme Court. It is worth noting that all the judges then in the federal court system had been appointed either by Washington or Adams, the first two presidents. Consequently, these judges were probably all Federalists and sympathetic to the outlook of the congressional majority, which also was dominated by Federalists.

When Thomas Jefferson was elected president in 1800, the Federalists lost control of Congress. The Alien and Sedition acts, which by their terms were to expire in 1801, were allowed by the new Congress to do so. President Jefferson pardoned everyone who had been convicted under the acts, and Congress appropriated money to refund fines that had been paid. These steps were taken in harmony with the new administration's view that the acts were unconstitutional.

The second time before 1912 that a free speech issue rose to national prominence was in *Patterson v. Colorado* 205 U.S. 454, a case the U.S. Supreme Court decided in 1907. Thomas Patterson, publisher of a Denver newspaper, was held in contempt of court by the Supreme Court of Colorado for disruption of the judicial process. His offense consisted of critical reporting of alleged "shenanigans" on the part of a majority of that court's justices in attempting to remove one or two justices the majority found politically objectionable. The U.S. Supreme Court, in the best tradition of Blackstone, affirmed Patterson's conviction saying, "In the first place, the main purpose of [the First Amendment] is 'to prevent all such *previous restraints* upon publications as had been practiced by other governments,' and [it does] not prevent the subsequent punishment [of acts that] may be deemed contrary to the public welfare" (205 U.S. 454, 462).

No further case was presented to the U.S. Supreme Court in which the court even suggested modification of this narrow interpretation of the amendment until the 1931 case of *Near v. Minnesota,* 283 U.S. 691 (1931), in which the court suggested that the First Amendment might have a wider reach. Beginning with that case, the pendulum has swung in the other direction, the Alien and Sedition acts being generally now thought to have been unconstitutional, and the reasoning of the *Patterson* case to have been wrong. But this change in judicial thinking did not come until almost twenty years after adoption of the 1912 Radio Act.

The fact that so few people were involved in wireless in any way might also have been a factor in the attitude of Congress toward wireless regulation. Because such regulation would have affected only a tiny fraction of the population, no political uproar was to be anticipated, and none in fact occurred. If a court *had* been faced with a First Amendment challenge to licensing in 1912, it might have analyzed the question in quite different terms than if such case were to have been presented to the same court in, say, 1934, when the proportion of the population regularly listening to radio was substantially higher. As it turned out, the court has never been *required* to consider whether need of a license to broadcast infringes First Amendment rights. Consequently, the court has never answered that question following a full, adversarial debate of the issue.

In any event, the 1912 act became law and required a federal license to engage in sending messages through the electromagnetic spectrum. The country seemed to "accept" as natural such a requirement. Indeed, the major broadcasters in the 1920s were as firm as anyone else in their support of federal regulation. Their concern at that time was with signal interference, a consequence of overcrowding of broadcast facilities and a problem for which the license requirement provided a solution.

As to the effectiveness of the 1912 act, the license requirement in its early days was more honored in the breach than in the observance. Congress failed to appropriate adequate monies for policing, with the result that enforcement was weak. Perhaps many amateur operators may have been unaware that a license was required of them. Others, even though aware of the act, probably couldn't believe their amateur operations were important enough to require obtaining a license from the secretary of commerce in Washington, D.C. For whatever reason, the requirement of a license to broadcast was widely ignored, and Congress did not again take up questions concerning regulation of the electromagnetic spectrum until 1927.

War broke out in Europe in 1914, but the United States did not become a combatant until Congress declared war on Germany in 1917. Meanwhile the United States Navy had been preparing for a possible role in the conflict. Crises created by German U-boat activities, preceding and following U.S. entry into the war, underlined the importance of wireless and intensified the determination of navy leaders to develop and control use of that technology within the United States. Although the navy was not to gain such control, its involvement after the war as a participant in use of wireless was of immeasurable importance in determining the direction taken by broadcasting.

In the course of its preparation for possible participation in World War I, the navy still had been unable to find a system of wireless communication as satisfactory as that available through American Marconi. In fact, it had not found a system that could be dubbed "satisfactory" at all: The American Marconi system remained unacceptable because of the conditions attached to its use by British Marconi and was considered "foreign owned." Notwithstanding American Marconi's incorporation under the laws of an American state, that corporation was considered to represent British interests, and the navy had no wish to be dependent upon a communications system controlled by a foreign country.

Although Congress had enacted the Radio Act of 1912 in part to protect certain parts of the spectrum for naval use without risk of interference, such protection was not intended and could not bring into being a system to satisfy naval needs. In fact, the technological development of radio, which might produce a solution to the navy's problems, had been stalled by another body of federal law, that is, patent law, under which numerous roadblocks had been erected in the form of patent claims covering even the most obscure areas of wireless technology. American entry into the war finally gave the navy the opportunity to cut through these obstacles to resolve its dilemma.

Only days after U.S. entry into World War I, deriving its power from the emergency, the navy took possession of all American Marconi facilities and instructed all suppliers of radio equipment to the navy to ignore all patent restrictions or disputes while the war lasted. The government, said the directive, would hold such suppliers harmless in connection with patent infringement claims. The navy hoped to encourage development of wireless communication equipment at least as good as that used by Marconi, preferably better.

America's entry into the war provided another boost to radio's fortunes. Military requirements called for training thousands of new people in the use and maintenance of wireless equipment, which undoubtedly awakened an urge in many to engage in some kind of activity involving radio after the war. Thus were the ranks of those with an interest in the future of this technology greatly increased.

CHAPTER 3

RCA

Technological progress in the wireless field during the war, and the navy's impatience with British control of the only viable wireless system, combined soon after the war's end to bring about transfer of control of the developing use of wireless technology in the United States from the British-dominated American Marconi corporation to an American corporation specifically created for that purpose.

In 1918, the war having ended, American Marconi renewed its earlier proposal to GE to buy Alexanderson alternators, the most powerful transmitting equipment available. The purchase price offered was $5 million. As before, Marconi was to have exclusive rights to use the alternator in wireless telecommunication. Five million dollars was a tremendous sum of money, and GE was certainly interested, but the U.S. government was opposed to the arrangement. It wanted development of future wireless communication in the United States to be in American hands and continued to oppose strengthening the British position, which the government believed would result from the proposed deal. The navy particularly opposed British control of wireless communications. It did not want what was currently the best intership communication technology under the control of a foreign country but, in addition to having control of that technology, wanted the electromagnetic spectrum nationalized and its use placed under the navy's control.

A bill to accomplish the navy's objective had been introduced in Congress by Representative Joshua Alexander of Missouri. It encountered considerable hostility. During the war, national telephone operations, as well as control of some railroads, had been placed under government control as temporary war measures. Many believed the government's management of these activities to have been inept, a result detrimental to the idea of pub-

25

lic management of much of anything. This was also the era of the Bolshe-
vik revolution, which doubtless had a negative influence on proposals for
naval control of broadcasting. In the event, Alexander's bill never got out
of committee.

Another approach was undertaken by the Navy Department. Assistant
Secretary of the Navy Franklin D. Roosevelt, whether at the suggestion of
President Wilson or not is unclear, contacted Owen Young, a vice president and general counsel of GE. Roosevelt was certainly acting with the
knowledge of Navy Secretary Josephus Daniels in this contact to let Young
know that the government opposed the proposed sale of alternators to
Marconi. GE was anxious to move on the Marconi proposal because the
proposed transaction meant considerable profit to the corporation and
went far to establishing a continuing market for the alternator. Consequently, Young wanted a quick meeting with government representatives.
Admiral William Bullard and Commander Stanford Hooper were dis-
patched to meet with Young on April 8, 1919.

Young always maintained that he had received a letter from Wilson
encouraging formation of an American consortium to buy out the British
Marconi interests, and that Bullard and Hooper reiterated that position in
the meeting. No such letter has been found, and others have emphasized
that the two navy men simply conveyed to Young the government's opposition to the sale of alternators to Marconi and probably expressed interest
in a possible buyout of American Marconi from the British. Regardless of
what in fact occurred, Young concluded, probably not erroneously, that the
government spokesmen did not oppose a possible acquisition by GE of the
operations of American Marconi as a means to end British domination of
world communications. For Daniels control of wireless by a private corporation was undesirable, but if such control was unavoidable, he wanted the
controlling corporation to be American. The navy let it be known that if
GE was successful in taking over the position of American Marconi,
patents in radio technology acquired by the navy in anticipation of its control of radio would be transferred to the Marconi successor designated by
GE.

The upshot was that GE rejected Marconi's proposal and made a
counteroffer for GE to purchase all the British shares of American Marconi. When GE made its proposal, the United States still had not returned
to American Marconi its assets seized in 1917. In agreeing to the sale,
British Marconi may well have considered this inaction by the U.S. government as evidence the United States just might never agree to return
these properties to a "foreign-owned" corporation. GE's proposed stock

purchase was accepted, and in the fall of 1919 the Radio Corporation of America was incorporated in Delaware by GE to take over the assets and operations of American Marconi. Management of the new corporation remained the same as that of the predecessor. Edward Nally, chief operating officer of the old corporation, became president of RCA. Nally's chief assistant, David Sarnoff, was named commercial manager of RCA, and Owen Young became the new corporation's board chairman. As planned, patent rights held by American Marconi were added to those of GE and further augmented by those of the navy.

The agreement between GE and RCA provided not only for the exclusive cross-licensing of all their patents but also provided that GE would manufacture all radio components RCA needed in its business. The U.S. government was given the right to name a nonvoting observer to attend meetings of RCA's board of directors and promptly named Admiral Bullard to that role. The articles of incorporation also limited possible foreign ownership of RCA stock.

In testimony before Congress in 1927, after President Wilson was dead, Owen Young said that Roosevelt had delivered to him a letter from Wilson expressing the president's urgent wish to keep wireless technology in American hands (Case and Case 1982, 173). The president, Young went on, expressed his belief that to be a world power in the future, the United States would need secure use of sea lanes, access to petroleum reserves, and control of its communication facilities. GE, Young testified, had answered Wilson's call in a "spirit of patriotism," creating RCA for the purpose of eliminating British control of U.S. wireless through its domination of American Marconi. This account is believed by some and disbelieved by others. The letter Young referred to was not found, and such an approach by Wilson as Young described seemed to many to be out of character. Nonetheless, the monopoly that RCA and its corporate shareholders created was often pictured by its management as created at the request of the government—a picture that RCA found particularly useful to improve its image when it faced charges of unlawful monopolization of radio. Undoubtedly, the government encouraged elimination of American Marconi. To the extent GE's plan for creation of RCA to hold exclusive patent rights was understood by government officials as the means for eliminating Marconi, that plan, too, the government apparently accepted. This would seem to be true whether or not those government officials had a real understanding of the nature of the cartel that was being formed. GE did what it did for the benefit of its shareholders; if such action also pleased the government, all well and good.

The pooling of patents belonging to GE, the navy, and American Marconi did not fully realize GE's corporate objectives. Some patents capable of giving RCA trouble remained in third-party hands. De Forest's audion tube was an essential element. The regeneration and oscillation features of that tube, discovered and advanced by Armstrong (or De Forest, depending on one's view), were two of its vital characteristics. These last two inventions were being litigated by the two inventors, and no decision was in sight. AT&T had purchased De Forest's rights in 1915. Owen Young therefore turned his attention to AT&T.

In July 1920 Young and the chairman of AT&T signed an agreement under which AT&T was issued 1 million shares in RCA in exchange for AT&T's assigning to the RCA patent pool full and exclusive rights to exploit radio patents owned by AT&T. The cartel members, now GE, AT&T, and RCA, defined their various rights in exploitation of the commercial possibilities (as they then understood them) presented by wireless. AT&T was to have exclusive rights to use of the radio technology for purposes akin to those identified with the telephone, such uses denominated by the parties as "radio telephony." The phone company renounced any rights to use of such patents in telegraphy, RCA's primary business. No mention was made of any interest in broadcasting. In fact, when AT&T had purchased De Forest's audion rights, the inventor had reserved to himself, without objection from AT&T, the right to exploit the audion in broadcasting. Although this limited AT&T only with regard to De Forest, it is likely AT&T continued to take the position that it was not interested in such activity. For himself, De Forest never succeeded in marshaling sufficient resources to capitalize on the rights he had reserved.

Developments involving Westinghouse caused Owen Young to conclude that it, too, must be brought into the RCA fold. Westinghouse controlled some important rights, including the Armstrong patents relative to the regeneration and oscillation features of the audion it had acquired in 1920, as well as patents covering some of Fessenden's inventions. Westinghouse also owned the radio station that carried the first regularly scheduled programming, imitating the amateur transmissions of Frank Conrad, a Westinghouse engineer.

In his programs Frank Conrad often played records, leading listeners to request that Conrad play specific selections. Some department stores in Pittsburgh, becoming aware of Conrad's "programs," saw such requests as a possible means to increase sales of radios. So did a Westinghouse executive who concluded Westinghouse should get in on this kind of radio transmission to promote sales of radios it manufactured. Westinghouse consequently started its pioneering station in Pittsburgh in 1920, inaugurating broadcasting as we know it today.

Given what Westinghouse saw as its strengths, that corporation bargained hard with GE, its competitor, when approached to join the radio patent pool. Westinghouse's stance was rewarded by receipt of a million RCA shares and the commitment by RCA and GE that Westinghouse would supply 40 percent of RCA's needs for radio equipment, the balance to be furnished by GE. RCA, under the various agreements, was not going to have its own manufacturing facilities.

The fifth, and last, member to be added to this alliance was United Fruit Corporation. This seemingly unlikely participant had purchased wireless equipment from American Marconi to improve and modernize control over its Central American banana-growing operations. Some of the equipment proved unsatisfactory, provoking a dispute about monies due. To settle the claim, RCA, as Marconi's successor, issued stock to United Fruit and thereby gained its future purchase orders. Because United Fruit had an interest in further development of radio for use in Central America, and the RCA cartel was the most likely source of improvements, United Fruit also granted RCA exclusive rights in such radio patents as it had acquired in connection with its efforts to improve communication in its Central American operations.

One description of the resulting cartel was furnished in 1922 by Ewin L. Davis,[1] a member of the House of Representatives, who said on the House floor: "These companies, by an elaborate series of restraints written into these agreements, jointly conspired to monopolize the new art of radio, not only in the field of modern broadcasting, but in all other branches of this revolutionary art" (Ventura Free Press 1932, 32).

The agreements under which these corporations pooled all of the outstanding important patents relative to wireless, Davis continued, gave them control of all aspects of telegraph, telephone, and radio for a period not to end before 1945. Combined with the power derived from the billions of dollars behind them, this monopoly was one of unparalleled size and scope.

Author Robert Sobel characterized the birth of RCA as "nothing less than the [beginning] of what President Eisenhower . . . call[ed] 'the military-industrial complex,'" this firstborn member being an all-encompassing, national wireless corporation (Sobel 1986, 26).

And author Susan J. Douglas, in her *Inventing American Broadcasting, 1899-1922*, described the cartel as marking the end of an era of individual inventors as heroes and role models for American youth (Douglas 1987,

240). The ingenious inventors who brought to light the secrets of the electromagnetic spectrum for human use faded from memory as the products their invention had produced became identified with the names of the corporations exploiting that art.

The last half of the 19th century had seen the rise of the "robber barons," the ruthlessness of industrial moguls, the killing of working men struggling to escape the almost total control of their employing corporations (as in the Pullman strike), and a growing public anger over concentration of corporate power. In the last decades of the 19th century, reflecting the public's concern about the perceived evils of the growth of trusts and other monopolistic practices, Congress had enacted the Sherman and Clayton Antitrust acts. By the second decade of the twentieth century the public's intense interest in this area had faded, largely, according to Douglas, as a result of the treatment accorded business by the press. "The large newspaper's paradoxical role," wrote Douglas, "—[itself product of a] capitalist firm, built and dependent on technical advances, yet watchdog over the postwar industrial order—produced an ambivalence about industrialism [that was] reflected in its articles and headlines. The press straddled both the world of business and the arena of public perceptions" (Douglas 1987, xxiv).

The function of news media, she went on, then almost wholly confined to the printed press, revealed its ambivalence in its treatment of this "signal achievement of business and military," the creation of RCA. In recognition of the importance of that "signal" event, the press provided minimal coverage, described by Douglas as "[only one article] . . . on the subject listed in the *Reader's Guide* for 1919 or 1920. The New York *Times* printed a front-page story on January 5, 1920, headlined 'American Radio to Span the Globe,' which described RCA's purpose as managing an international wireless operating system that would compete with the cables (Douglas 1987, 288).

Through the years after RCA was born, both GE and RCA have played the patriotic line as good PR for their corporate image. Some have questioned the extent of the government's parentage in the birth of RCA, believing the two corporations guilty of embellishing history even if they did not fabricate it. There can be little doubt, however, that the navy did play some role in the creation of RCA, as a midwife at least. Navy patents surrendered to RCA were not "stolen." That GE's motivation in its purchase of Marconi stock and incorporation of RCA was not purely, perhaps even primarily, patriotic seems clear. Only a certain naïveté as to the nature of corporations and capitalism could sustain such a belief. GE management believed it could make money for its stockholders. If it could do this under a canopy of patriotism, so much the better. In the event, it played its hand well.

Nothing is perfect, though, and a relatively minor blip soon appeared. In 1924, acting on complaints from independent radio manufacturers like Emerson, Motorola, and Philco, the Federal Trade Commission began an inquiry into the trade practices of RCA. Started during the Harding administration (which was hardly antibusiness), the FTC's action was brought to an abrupt conclusion in 1928. The earlier commencement of that action, though, provided an unanticipated assist to resolving a major battle among the members of the RCA cartel, a battle that began in 1922 and was to threaten the future of radio. I now turn to the consideration of that dispute.

Notes

1. Author of the 1923 Davis Amendment to the Radio Act of 1927.

CHAPTER 4

RCA in Crisis

T he Radio Corporation of America, created by the cartel of five
with the cooperation, if not connivance, of the U.S. Navy, was to
a great extent simply a tool of the five. It had no manufacturing
facilities and was required to fill its needs for finished radios and radio parts
from cartel members. It was in effect an outlet for the others, delegated to
protect the cartel's patent interests from infringement by outsiders. RCA's
operations were accordingly considerably more circumscribed than were
those of independent business entities.

The battle among the members of the RCA cartel referred to at the
end of chapter 3 was centered in broadcasting, an activity that was becoming increasingly important, but one that had simply not been anticipated or dealt with in the various cartel agreements. How wireless was to
be used and by whom were major questions. A related question was how
any such use was to be financed. David Sarnoff, RCA's commercial manager, had some ideas on these subjects.

The name David Sarnoff, more than that of any other person, runs
like a thread through the history of American broadcasting. Neither inventor nor political figure, he wielded an influence like that of a founding
father's, which permeates any examination of how broadcasting came to be
what it is today.

Sarnoff was a businessman as much concerned with the "bottom line"
as anyone else, but he was also a visionary who conceived that broadcasting should be a public service. Radio, he believed, represented a powerful
force for influencing the listening public. Consequently, it occupied a place
that could give rise to potentially serious conflicts of interest between corporate responsibility in serving the profit motives of shareholders, and the
obligation to serve the interests of its listeners. Sarnoff presented to RCA's

board a proposal that he thought could resolve the conflict. It is doubtful
it would have done so, but he made the effort. As matters developed, his
ideas were never tested.

The new RCA board of directors named some of its members to serve
as a "broadcasting committee." In June of 1922 Sarnoff sent a letter to that
committee detailing his ideas concerning the future of broadcasting and
his conception of its responsibilities. The letter was an elaboration of the
1916 memo he had presented to American Marconi management.

Sarnoff described the obligations of broadcasting as entertaining , in-
forming, and educating the public. He placed emphasis on the first, but he
believed the last two were not to be taken lightly. He thought broadcasting
should be national in scope; only a few stations would be needed to fulfill
radio's role as he envisioned it. Local station development serving strictly
local issues was inconsistent with his ideas. He also considered that none
of the corporations making up the radio cartel controlling RCA were
equipped to undertake the responsibility of designing and producing programming. Rather, Sarnoff proposed that a nonprofit corporation, controlled by RCA, should be set up to perform these functions. Thus its programs would be designed to meet the public service criterion, not the goal
of maximizing corporate profits. This entity would be financed by contributions from each of the five members of the cartel, consisting of a percentage of revenues derived from the radio business.

Sarnoff recognized that this financing might prove inadequate and
hoped any shortfall would be met by persuading retail radio dealers to contribute a portion of their revenues as well. Additionally, enlightened persons of wealth might be induced to endow the nonprofit corporation, further adding to its financial strength.

RCA's broadcasting committee never responded to Sarnoff's proposal.
In the end, that probably didn't matter much; within a matter of weeks af-
ter Sarnoff wrote it, AT&T announced the establishment of radio station
WEAF, with a transmitter in the heart of Manhattan.

AT&T began working on the use of wireless for long-distance telephone service before 1915. In that year the telephone company, using an
improved audion and with the help of the navy, had succeeded in sustain-
ing brief voice contacts with Paris and Hawaii from a location at the U.S.
Navy's Arlington, Virginia, facility. Continuous efforts by AT&T labs had
since produced remarkable results, and the telephone company felt ready
in 1922 to cash in on its achievements.

In announcing the opening of WEAF, AT&T likened the station to a
phone booth for long-distance phone calls. Such calls would utilize the arts

of both wire and wireless. What AT&T intended was that the station should be considered a phone booth from which persons could send any message they wished to the public at large—for a fee, of course. Those interested, said the announcement, should contact the local AT&T long-distance phone service manager, who, in addition to making the necessary arrangements for the station's use, could help in assuring that the proposed message would be suitable, that is, would not offend any sizable portion of the listening public. Even then it was evident that the owner of the transmitter was in the business of "delivering an audience," a business AT&T did not propose to damage by allowing programming identified with its call letters to be offensive to those being addressed.

Interestingly, when AT&T released this announcement inviting the world of commerce to enter a new arena of salesmanship, no "takers" stepped forward. So AT&T undertook to be salesman to the salesmen, sending reps into the field to drum up business for the new transmitter. The first customer was a Queens, New York, real estate development company that bought ten minutes to pitch its projects either as an investment or as providing a residence. Sponsored programming had arrived; the source of funds to support broadcasting had been identified. Although the operation of WEAF got off to a slow start, its activity grew steadily. It was a success.

When AT&T announced the availability of WEAF for commercial programs, it also informed its fellow cartel members that in future none of them would be permitted to use phone lines for the transmission of programs. AT&T also announced that, as it read the cartel agreements, only AT&T could be compensated for use of broadcasting facilities, because it alone could operate "radio telephony"—with emphasis on the "telephony." These actions by AT&T were seen by some as an attempt to destroy RCA.

WEAF's equipment was top-notch. Its transmitter was the best available, its signals the loudest and clearest then heard. Location of the station in midtown New York made it accessible to professional entertainers of all stripes— individuals who were then eager to appear as unpaid guests on radio programs simply for the exposure. Competing stations operated by Westinghouse and General Electric were inconvenient, and none provided transportation to the outreaches of New Jersey, or wherever. Clarity of their signal was inferior, and the source of funds to support programs had been made uncertain by AT&T's claim that only it could receive compensation for broadcasting services—a claim that had some support in the language of the agreements. The other members of the cartel, and particularly RCA, were thrown into turmoil.

Denial of use of the phone lines had an immediate impact. WJZ, operating from its New Jersey location, had planned to broadcast baseball's 1922 World Series. Without the phone lines, play-by-play description of the game could not be relayed from the game's site to the transmitter. WJZ made emergency arrangements for use of Western Union lines. Though this alternative solved the immediate crisis, it was a temporary expedient because Western Union lines would not generally be available, and, more important, they provided nowhere near the quality for voice transmission of AT&T's phone lines.

Owen Young and other cartel members began negotiations with AT&T in an attempt to end the cartel's civil war quickly. AT&T viewed its position as strong, and little progress was made. The parties agreed to hire an independent lawyer to analyze the cartel agreements and evaluate the claims of each side. The resulting opinion gave AT&T some comfort but also supported some of the others' conclusions. Arbitration was considered, but the final decision would have to be accepted in advance, so neither side found this solution a very attractive idea, doubtful as the outcome was. In 1924 the Federal Trade Commission filed a complaint against the cartel members, giving the contestants additional incentive to resolve their dispute.

The FTC action resulted from complaints of independent radio manufacturers such as Philco, Motorola, and Emerson that RCA and its corporate owners were guilty of unfair trade practices in monopolizing the production of radios and radio parts. One of the sources of the high income being generated by the radio sector of RCA's business, which was run by David Sarnoff, was patent fees. To the best of his ability, Sarnoff saw to it that the patents in the patent pool were used by outsiders only if royalties demanded by RCA were paid. Sarnoff also determined the amount of royalties—which, in each case, was high. In furtherance of enforcement efforts, RCA created a patent "police" force that combed retail stores and manufacturing facilities to prevent bootleg radios from being put on the market without patent payments. Independent manufacturers found competing with RCA under these conditions tough. They considered themselves gouged, and the FTC agreed.

One consequence of the FTC complaint was that Sarnoff lowered the royalty rates for independents. Another was that AT&T accelerated a move it had begun earlier to divest itself of RCA stock. Finally, and inevitably, the phone giant became more serious about trying to settle the cartel's internal disputes that its own maneuvering had engendered. In 1926 a peace agreement was reached that was so simple; it suggests that AT&T was no longer greatly interested in the type of broadcasting it had started with its "wireless phone booth."

Under the settlement, RCA bought WEAF for $1 million, and AT&T reserved the right to engage in future broadcasting. If AT&T did decide to resume broadcasting, however, it would have to refund the million dollars to RCA. With AT&T thus effectively out of broadcasting, the remaining issues were rapidly resolved. Phone lines would be available at competitive rates, and any broadcaster could derive revenue any way it wished. AT&T reserved the right to resume broadcasting, but to date it has not done so.

As with so much that was decisive in the history of broadcasting, Sarnoff's participation in the negotiations was of much importance. The settlement was along lines he had suggested some years before its consummation.

Successful termination of the war with AT&T over WEAF, in combination with the ideas put forth by Sarnoff in his 1922 letter to RCA's broadcasting committee, led to the creation of a subsidiary of RCA, the National Broadcasting Company (NBC). This company would provide the network for RCA, controlling programming on stations owned by cartel members and, as it later developed, on independent affiliates. Part of Sarnoff's vision was then realized, even if the other major ingredient of ensuring operation as a public service was not. Of course, today's networks and broadcasters contend that their programming provides a public service, and that any "conflict of interest" charge is nonsense in light of the high number of broadcasters and other media outlets operating within a competitive market. They also claim to be subject to a strong tradition in journalism (with which they identify themselves) known as the separation of "church" and "state." This separation prevents the "state," the business arm concerned with profit, from pressuring the "church," the repository of independent editorial judgment. The "church" part, relieved of worry about profits, single-mindedly devotes itself to serving the public interest, without need to be concerned if a heavy advertiser like Ford Motor Company is disturbed by reports of defects in its product.[1] Finally, they grumble, there is some government oversight of broadcasting operations by the FCC—an oversight that is not without *some* effect on licensee performance.

Owen Young recommended to RCA's board that one Merlin Aylesworth be named president of NBC. Aylesworth, a former executive in the electric utility industry, had expressed the view that "public" utilities formed part of a communist conspiracy. Though Aylesworth appeared to have views philosophically at odds with David Sarnoff's, Sarnoff voiced no objection to Young's suggestion, and Aylesworth became head of NBC. After all, from Sarnoff's point of view, WEAF had ended the "public service" role for NBC visualized in his 1922 letter.

Additional insight into views Aylesworth brought to broadcasting can be gained by examining various comments he made after joining NBC. He once described his understanding of the role of advertising in programming: "Broadcast advertising," he said, "is unique in that its advertising and editorial copy are combined in the sponsored program. The two are blended in a perfect union." In an appearance before a trade group, Aylesworth said about himself that as a newcomer to the industry, starting, as he put it, "at the bottom of the top," he early on grasped, and indeed welcomed, the distinguishing feature of commercial network programming—the integration of advertising and content. He spoke glowingly of the process as "tacitly and unconsciously coupling the editorial or program features which appeal to us with the advertising message they contain." He went on to define the task of the continuity writer as "weaving the advertising motif into the warp and woof of entertainment" (Bergreen 1980, 58).

United States v. RCA

First came the FTC, then the Justice Department.

In May 1930, on his way to a dinner at the Manhattan apartment of a member of the RCA board of directors, Sarnoff, having within days been named RCA's new president, was accosted by a U.S. marshal who stepped out of shadows to serve him with a copy of the complaint filed that day in federal court in *The United States v. RCA, AT&T, General Electric Corp., United Fruit Corp., Westinghouse Electric Corp., et al.* This suit was an attempt by the Justice Department, responding to public concerns about the "radio monopoly," to break up the cartel, creation of which the government had at the very least encouraged in 1919. For the Hoover administration there was a political problem; many thought the administration too "probusiness" in the midst of depression. An election year, too, was not far off. For the antitrust gurus in the Justice Department, the main legal issue presented by the radio cartel was that the cross-licensing agreements, covering virtually all important patents dealing with radio technology, limited use of those patents to cartel members.

To David Sarnoff the government's action threatened the very existence of RCA. He saw that the easy way out for the non-RCA members of the cartel could be the dismantling of RCA with each cartel member resuming its original position. Fortunately for RCA and himself, Sarnoff was able to persuade both Owen Young, chairman of GE's board, and Judge Warren Olney, who represented the Justice Department, that survival of a healthy RCA was important. Given such backing, and Sarnoff's usual concentration of effort when mastering all aspects of litigation, his grasp of the issues enabled him to talk circles around other, less well-prepared cartel spokespersons and to turn aside threats to RCA. It was one of Sarnoff's greatest victories.

Under the consent decree by which the suit was ended and entered as a judgment in federal court in November 1932, the three corporate stockholders in RCA agreed to divest themselves of at least 50 percent of their RCA stock holdings. (AT&T had in prior years undertaken to divest itself of RCA stock and finished the job when the antitrust suit was filed.) The stockholders further agreed (as did AT&T) that the patent license agreements would become nonexclusive as to all parties. GE and Westinghouse would no longer require RCA to obtain components from their manufacturing facilities and would not even try to supply such components for a specified period. This allowed RCA to develop its own manufacturing capabilities.

Apart from the antitrust decree, the radio stations owned by GE and Westinghouse were leased to NBC for operation, and the debts owed by RCA to the former corporate shareholders were renegotiated on terms Sarnoff considered favorable to RCA.

Instead of causing the death of RCA, the federal lawsuit gave it new life. Possessed at last of complete independence, and with as solid a financial base as RCA could reasonably have hoped for, David Sarnoff commented, "They handed me a lemon. I made lemonade."

One price Sarnoff did have to pay. His good friend, Owen Young, who had supported Sarnoff in many hard times, was required by the consent decree to end his relationship with RCA. He could no longer be a director of the corporation, much less the board's chairman. Merlin Aylesworth, who had been selected by Young to be NBC's president, decided he, too, would leave. He had no desire to become, as he put it, "Sarnoff's boy!" In fact, Aylesworth remained at NBC until 1936, when he moved to RKO in an executive capacity.

In the next chapter I leave RCA and turn to the early 1920s to consider problems arising from increased use of the spectrum, as well as varied attempts to overcome them.

Notes

1. The *Los Angeles Times* recently adopted a variation of the church/state form that some might consider its abolition. A spokesperson for the "state" was assigned to each "church" department to keep it apprised of the financial aspects of its activities.

CHAPTER 5

Chaos Comes to Broadcasting

S ome historians of the period have estimated that at the end of 1920 there were fewer than 50,000 wireless receivers in the hands of the public, whereas just 13 months later there were between 600,000 and 1 million such sets. Thus had radio grown since World War I. Much of that growth must be attributed to the explosion of use by amateurs like Frank Conrad, leading to broadcasts by department stores selling radios, and then by radio manufacturers like Westinghouse.

Notwithstanding reservation under the 1912 act of certain frequencies for government use, interference with signals still plagued the military and was even more troublesome to private licensees. As the number of licensed "broadcasters" grew to exceed the spectrum's capacity to provide all with a clear signal, interference continued to be attributed primarily to amateurs. Even though amateurs had been restricted under the 1912 act to use of the spectrum at 200 meters and below—the least desirable frequencies—Congress had failed to adequately finance policing needed to ensure compliance with frequency allocations. Amateurs had quickly found they could operate up to a range of 475 meters without getting into trouble, and in 1920 they were still far and away the dominant users of radio.

Reacting to the chaos in broadcasting, Secretary of Commerce Hoover invited representatives of some broadcasting interests to attend a conference to be convened in Washington in 1922 for the purpose of considering how the signal interference problem might be resolved. Fifteen delegations attended, representing AT&T, Western Electric Corporation (an AT&T subsidiary), Westinghouse, General Electric, and RCA, along with several government agencies and fewer than a dozen other private entities.[1] Broadcast licenses had been granted to educational, civic, and religious institutions, but apparently none of them had been invited, nor did any attend.

Hoover opened the conference February 27 with a statement of his understanding of the meeting's purpose:

> This conference has been called at the request of the President and its purpose is to inquire into the critical situation that has arisen through the astonishing development of the wireless telephone, to advise the Department of Commerce as to the application of its present powers of regulation and to develop the situation generally with a view to some recommendation to Congress, if it be necessary, to extend the present powers of regulation. This is one of the few instances that I know of in this country where the public—all of the people interested—are unanimously for an extension of regulatory powers on the part of the Government. (U.S. Department of Commerce 1922, 2)

Hoover expressed what he conceived to be general agreement that use of wireless could not be devoted primarily to communication between individuals in the manner of the telephone. Rather, he said:

> I think it will be agreed . . . that the wireless telephone has one definite field, and that is for spread of certain pre-determined material of public interest from central stations. This material must be limited to news, to education, to entertainment, and the communication of such commercial matters as are of importance to large groups of the community at the same time. . . .
>
> It is therefore primarily a question of broadcasting, and it becomes of primary public interest to say who is to do the broadcasting, under what circumstances, and with what type of material. It is inconceivable that we should allow so great a possibility for service, for news, for entertainment, for education, and for vital commercial purposes, to be drowned in advertising chatter, or for commercial purposes that can be quite well served by our other means of communication. (U.S. Department of Commerce 1922, 2-3)

If Hoover was correct that there was general agreement that wireless should be devoted to broadcasting, the prevailing thinking would mark a 180-degree turn from the thinking of RCA's founders in 1920. It would also mirror the ideas David Sarnoff had expressed in his famous 1916 memo to Marconi management, ideas reiterated in the letter he wrote to members of RCA's board in June of 1922, about four months *after* the Radio Conference. From the reaction, or lack thereof, of RCA's board to that June letter, it is likely Hoover was overstating the consensus.

Hoover's reference to "unanimous" support by "those interested" in more government regulation also seems to have been an overstatement. He must have thought RCA agreed with him, yet other events occurring at the time make it doubtful such a belief was justified. Remarks by some of the cartel-member spokesmen did indicate support for regulatory action by government, and no clear opposition was heard. According to the minutes, though, the only spokesman for RCA didn't say much. Nonetheless, not long after the conference had concluded, sentiment favoring government regulation of some sort appeared to be unanimous so far as the large corporations were concerned. As for the thousands of individual operators, it is difficult to see how Hoover could have had any idea of their views.

The first speaker following Secretary Hoover at the conference was one A. H. Griswold of AT&T. He told the meeting that AT&T was in the process of setting up a service combining telephone and radio (U.S. Department of Commerce 1922, 5). It would, he said, operate like a public phone booth: Anyone wishing to use the service would pay AT&T and be able to send a message into the ether to be heard by anyone with receiving capability. In an apparent reference to the future WEAF, Griswold said that users would likely want to advertise some products to justify the cost of using the "phone booth." In other words, AT&T proposed to sell broadcast time. If this disturbed Mr. Hoover in light of his expressed disapproval of advertising, he did not say so.

When Hoover spoke of broadcasting as activity that should serve "the public interest," he could not have known that those words would later make up part of the standard for government action in regulating broadcasting under both the Federal Radio and the Communications acts. It is difficult to take exception to a goal to "serve the public interest." However, determining precisely what compliance with that goal means has proved enormously difficult. Does the public interest require that anyone wanting to broadcast be permitted to do so, or that some must be denied that right? Should program content be of any concern to the government? To listeners? If the answer to the latter is yes, how are listeners to make their concerns known? How are they to be fulfilled?

At the Radio Conferences little time was devoted to analyzing what the "public interest" required. But not surprisingly, many delegates were convinced that such interest was satisfied by what they did. Mr. L. R. Krumm, representing Westinghouse, which operated the only existing broadcasting station with regularly scheduled programs, said of Westinghouse's broadcast objectives:

> We have endeavored in the operation of our station to supply the demands of the public. We have always kept in mind that it was not our end of it that was valuable; it is what is received—how the man that receives it views it that determines whether our service is valuable. . . . Whereas fifty or a hundred or a thousand want to broadcast there are a million people [who] want to receive. . . . As against [the programming we provide at very large expense], it is perfectly possible to establish a so-called broadcasting station for about $500 or $1,000 initial investment, and the entertainment outlay represents nothing but phonograph records, and that sort of a station can interfere very disastrously with such a station as we are trying to operate, and that I think is the prime question before this committee. I think in [regulating broadcasting] . . . you have to keep in mind the [interests of] the receiver more than the wishes of the few people that desire to broadcast. . . . There is a limitation to the number of broadcasting stations that can operate successfully, and if you are going to get the desired results there must be some regulation and possibly limitation of the number of these stations.

Krumm added that Westinghouse programming was of the highest quality: "Our evening entertainments now contain no canned or phonograph entertainment; we confine ourselves to original entertainment, grand operas from Chicago, etc. We have taken this thing very seriously" (U.S. Department of Commerce 1922, 33-34). Providing such programming on a scheduled basis was very expensive, Krumm reiterated, and though Westinghouse wished to continue such broadcasting, the corporation also wanted to know the likelihood that its programs would remain free from signal interference.

The Westinghouse spokesman deplored the inexpensive and unimaginative broadcasting of "phonograph records." He probably never conceived of "talk" radio. His thrust was that sophisticated programming, necessarily expensive to produce, obviously served the public interest, whereas "cheap" shows did not. Of course, a commitment to produce such programs required an assurance of a clear frequency, and the Westinghouse station should be able to count on a license of long duration—how long

Krumm did not say. But he certainly voiced here one concept of "public interest." Over the years many have expressed ideas that have been variations of Krumm's, though others have been quite different.

In response to questions from government representatives, Krumm said that Westinghouse did not charge for its broadcasts. However, the company's motivations were not totally disinterested; Westinghouse did expect its broadcasts to build demand for the receivers it manufactured for distribution by RCA. Whether other product sales might be helped, Krumm could not say.

Three more Radio Conferences were sponsored by the Commerce Department, one each year from 1922 through 1925. Although verbatim minutes of conferences after the first were not published, conference recommendations were. Those attending the later conferences differed little from the cast in 1922; the interests of those attending got the ear of the secretary and were memorialized in the written records. Presumably at least some members of Congress read these records; so, perhaps, did some members of the press. Such readers would have been likely to conclude that the views expressed took into account the interests of all sorts of broadcasters in the United States. This conclusion would almost certainly have been erroneous, as evidenced by historical facts explored by Robert W. McChesney in his book, *Telecommunications, Mass Media, and Democracy,* published in 1994.

In the account of the 1925 Radio Conference, *Proceedings of the Fourth National Radio Conference and Recommendations for Regulation of Radio,* Hoover divided the problems of broadcasting into those that the industry could and should solve for itself, and those that could be resolved only by joint action of broadcasters and government. In the former category he placed station interconnections, advertising, and location. In the latter category he placed the problem of the limited number of frequencies then available for broadcasting. "We must face the actualities frankly," Hoover said. "We can no longer deal on the basis that there is room for everybody on the radio highways. There are more vehicles on the roads than can get by, and if they continue to jam in all will be stopped. . . . It is not a question of what we would like to do but what we must do" (*Proceedings* 1925, 6).

He then expressed a concern that probably elicited little sympathy in corporate board rooms. Although suggestions were made to increase the number of available frequencies by widening the broadcasting band, Hoover believed most radios then in use couldn't pick up programs transmitted at the higher frequencies that such widening would require. "Nor," he said, "could we extend [the band] without invading the field assigned to the amateurs, of whom there are thousands and to whose constant experimentation radio development is so greatly indebted. . . . [Amateur radio] has . . . a part in the fine development of the American boy, and I do not believe anyone will wish to minimize his part in American life." Widening the band, then, seemed out, as did taking frequencies away from "the American boy" to satisfy growing commercial demand. However, such sentimentality was no match for the power of commercial broadcasting in its drive to take control of the spectrum.

Turning his attention to questions of free speech, Hoover said:

> We hear a great deal about the freedom of the air; but there are two parties to freedom of the air, and to freedom of speech, for that matter. There is the speechmaker and the listener. Certainly in radio I believe in freedom for the listener. He has much less option upon what he can reject, for the other fellow is occupying his receiving set. The listener's only option is to abandon his right to use his receiver. Freedom can not mean a license to every person or corporation who wishes to broadcast his name or his wares, and thus monopolize the listener's set. (*Proceedings* 1925, 7)

The complex considerations voiced by Hoover certainly cut two ways. It is a pity that he did not proceed further with his analysis. Hoover was in essence supporting the views previously expressed by Westinghouse's Krumm: that control of broadcasting should rest with the "generalist" rather than with representatives of "special interests," with the large corporation rather than with the small organization or the individual. On the other hand, Hoover's words also deal something of a blow to "free market" theorists who believe that the public influences programming significantly through market forces. Some of Hoover's statements can be read as indication that he believed the role of government should be limited to that of a traffic cop, preventing signal interference. Other statements seem to go further, expressing concern about the content of broadcast programming. The commerce secretary never seems to have developed a clear picture as to what he thought serving the "public interest" required.

Problems of signal interference grew. Hoover came to believe that action by the government was necessary to sort out the mess into which broadcasting was descending. However, his preliminary attempts to assert some power to impose order had been rebuffed by the United States District Court for the District of Columbia. In a 1923 decision (*Hoover v. Intercity Radio Co.,* 286 Fed. 803), that court said the commerce secretary had no power under the 1912 act to refuse to issue a broadcast license to any applicant qualified under the act, notwithstanding the secretary's determination that the license sought would inevitably result in interference with signals of other licensees. Hoover then attempted to nurture a system of voluntary restraint on the part of broadcasters. That failing, and Hoover, perhaps, hoping the district court decision would be considered wrong, or of limited application, he resumed efforts at compulsory regulation with respect to the chaos problem. He adopted rules limiting broadcasters' rights to use of designated frequencies, apportioning broadcast time so that licensees could share common frequencies, and limiting transmission power for broadcaster use.

Subsequently, Zenith Radio Corporation was issued a license from the Commerce Department that restricted Zenith to certain hours of operation and to a specific frequency. Zenith ignored the frequency limit, and in 1926 lawyers for the Commerce Department brought a criminal action against Zenith for violating its license conditions. The federal court dismissed the case, deciding, as had the earlier court, that the secretary of commerce had no discretionary powers under the act, so no power to confine Zenith to a particular frequency (*U.S. v. Zenith Radio Corp.,* 12 F.2d 614, N.D., Ill.). This decision brought to an end the secretary's attempts to channel the development of broadcasting in a manner that would eliminate signal interference.

Hoover has been described as "adamant in his belief in the superiority of having broadcasting 'in the hands of private enterprise,'" and believing that "'those directly engaged in radio, particularly in broadcasting, should be able, to a very large extent, to regulate and govern themselves'" (McChesney 1994, 13). Though this may be true, it could be a result, at least in part, of the two court decisions that had undercut Hoover's efforts to impose a more general order on the industry, legally correct though those two decisions may have been.

The picture of Hoover that emerges is that of a naive man, committed to the interests of private commercial business, who could not bring himself to believe that the people he knew in business would disagree with his vision of the importance of broadcasting. He also demonstrated no curiosity about noncommercial possibilities within broadcasting aside from the activities of "amateurs," sentimentally regarded by him as the "American boy."

Notes

1. Other identified participants were Pacific Radio Trade Association, Ship Owners' Radio Service, American Radio Relay League (an association of amateur operators), Federal Telephone and Telegraph Company, Radio Committee of National Electric Light Association, Boy Scouts of America, Philadelphia Police Department, Detroit News, National Retail Dry Goods Association, De Forest Telephone and Telegraph Company, Precision Equipment Company, Radio Electric Company, U.S. Shipping Board Emergency Fleet Corporation, United States Public Health Service, and I.R. Nelson Company.

CHAPTER 6

The Radio Act of 1927

C ongress finally responded to urging from Hoover and many broadcasters in 1927 by adopting the Federal Radio Act, which created a Radio Commission with a life of one year. Composed of five members appointed by the president, the commission was charged with imposing order on use of the electromagnetic spectrum by reviewing all broadcast licenses already granted. It was empowered to revoke existing licenses, review applications for new licenses, and issue licenses with such conditions as it might determine necessary to accomplish its mission. Congress assumed the commission would complete its work in one year, and the act contemplated a transfer of the commission's routine functions to the Commerce Department upon expiration of the one-year term. However, that period proved inadequate for completion of the review of existing licenses, and the commission's life was thereafter extended by Congress from year to year until 1934, when the Federal Communications Act was passed to replace the 1927 Radio Act.

The 1927 legislation, which required that commission decisions serve the "public interest, convenience, and necessity," had been complicated less than a year after passage of the Radio Act, when Congress amended it by passing the Davis Amendment, named for its sponsor, Ewin L. Davis, a member of the House from Tennessee. This legislation divided the country into five sections and ordered the commission to arrange broadcast transmission facilities so that each section would be more or less equally served. Sometimes the commission wavered between enforcing the purposes of the amendment and the requirement to serve the "public interest," but nothing told them which of these sets of commands was paramount. The intent of the Davis Amendment might be considered an attempt to treat each of the five regions more or less equally in terms of the grant of broadcast licenses and location of broadcast facilities. However, the unpredictably vagrant quality of broadcast signals, combined with factors like the location of population centers, might reasonably lead to the conclusion that unequal treatment better serves the "public interest," at least so far as the maximization of clear signal transmission to the greatest number of listeners is concerned.

During its lifetime the Radio Commission accomplished most of its assigned tasks. It gave a temporary extension to all licenses issued under the 1912 act before undertaking to review the broadcasting "web" throughout the country for the purpose of deciding which stations should be continued. Many licenses ultimately were revoked or not renewed, and the total number of operating stations was reduced by about a third. Except as they felt constrained by the Davis Amendment, the commissioners viewed their job primarily as one of engineering—that is, they were to optimize use of the spectrum by ensuring, insofar as possible, that there would be clear signals throughout the country and a minimum of interference. Except with respect to what they considered obviously objectionable programming (and some programming fit that bill, as we will later see), they did not concern themselves with program content when considering the public interest.

As successor to the Radio Act, the Communications Act inaugurated regulation of telephone service and rates, all under the authority of a new agency, the Federal Communications Commission, which replaced the Radio Commission. Membership on the Communications Commission was increased to seven, and the agency was made a permanent part of the government. Most other provisions of the Communications Act were identical to those of the Radio Act[1].

Major winners under both laws were the corporations that had joined together to form the Radio Corporation of America. Most of the losers were noncommercial and small radio operators. In the final analysis, the airwaves thereafter were dominated by the major winners. Historians of broadcasting disagree as to whether genuine opportunity existed during the decade preceding adoption of the Communications Act for development of a strong noncommercial presence in broadcasting. In his book *Telecommunications, Mass Media, and Democracy,* Robert McChesney provides detailed documentation of his thesis that a strong role for noncommercial radio was still possible until 1934. Only then, he contends, did any serious possibility of meaningful noncommercial broadcasting in America evaporate. Whether McChesney is right or wrong, the final outcome seems inevitable in light of decisions of the Radio Conferences that helped to define Radio Commission policies favoring commercial broadcasting and the dominance of the RCA cartel. These were the people, after all, with the greatest engineering expertise, able to demonstrate an ability to project strong, clear signals to large audiences.

Other developments occurring years before adoption of the Communications Act suggest that the chances for noncommercial broadcasting were slim. Broadcast licenses were issued by the Radio Commission for a term of three months. As a license came up for renewal, the commission allowed competitors to oppose renewal and urge that the license be transferred to themselves. Such contests were generally restricted to cases in which large corporations or independent applicants affiliated with a network opposed renewal attempts by smaller stations. The only noncommercial broadcasters were small stations. Licenses held by commercial interests seldom faced renewal opposition when their terms expired.

By the time the Communications Commission became the licensing agency, most small and part-time broadcasters had lost their licenses, although many had been promised that the successor network licensee or affiliate would "provide them with broadcast time." Although it is impossible to determine the bona fides of such promises at this late date, under depression conditions these assurances may well have been sincere. The percentage of the nation's production capacity actually in use was at an all-time low, as was demand for radio advertising time. Educational, religious, or other community-service organizations may have seemed just the ticket to fill nonsponsored time slots and to offer the licensed station programming with substantial goodwill value. In any case the promises were apparently incapable of being enforced and increasingly went unfulfilled.

In granting licenses and adopting such regulations as deemed necessary to control broadcasting, the Radio Commission, as previously noted, was required to serve the public interest. A comparable standard had commonly been used in the regulation of public utilities. Permission to operate a transit company or to provide additional electric power in a particular area could well be decided on the basis of whether such addition was "in the public interest." Considerations like existing demand, costs, and the effect on consumers of having the additional (or original) service authorized would all be relevant, but the usefulness of such a standard as a guide for decision making in the complex area of broadcasting has been questioned by many.

The Radio Act's public interest standard was variously defined. Larger stations, all of which considered themselves disinterested, argued that the standard was met by the programming of disinterested broadcasters. Such broadcasters, they argued, were more likely to provide coverage of a wide range of matter and outlooks than were smaller stations. Small stations, the argument went, would as a rule represent narrow points of view. Like the station operated by the AFL-CIO, they could be expected to have an "ax to grind." The networks called such broadcasters "propaganda" stations, assigning them a descriptive adjective the Radio Commission itself ultimately adopted to identify many smaller stations. However, another possible interpretation of "public interest" was simply that the listening public should receive clear signals without interference. This standard implied fewer rather than more licensees. Finally, because better-financed producers could provide greater variety in programming than could those with fewer resources, some argued that the former should be favored as licensees "in the interest of the public."

In April 1927 one of the first members of the new Radio Commission, Henry A. Bellows, said in a speech to the League of Women Voters:

> Above all, it is for you, not for us of the commission, to safe-guard the so-called freedom of the air. Here is a problem which, because you are primarily interested in radio as a means of political education, touches you very closely. You would be quick to see the danger if there could be only a fixed and rather small number of newspapers and magazines published in the United States; you would rightly fear that the newcomer, the nonconformist, the representative of the minority, would have small chance to present his ideas to the public. This is just the situation which exists in broadcasting and which inevitably must continue to exist unless some fundamental change in the science of radio transmission comes about as the result of new discovery, to make possible a totally unforeseen increase in the number of stations which can broadcast simultaneously. (*First Annual* 1971, 7)

Bellows, who after leaving the Radio Commission was hired by CBS to head its government affairs section, went on to say that only a few may be accorded the right to broadcast because of the limitations of the spectrum. The immediate job of safeguarding free speech essential to intellectual growth, he continued, lies first in the hands of the broadcasters, but ultimately rests with listeners because it is their goodwill that the broadcasters seek. Failing both, he concluded, the government might feel compelled to regulate broadcast programming.

Bellows's comments seem unusual; we normally think of freedom of speech as a right of the *speaker* with which government may not interfere.

Yet Bellows tells the *listeners* that they, rather than the commission, must safeguard "freedom of the air" to be sure that they *receive* the political information they need—as though listeners too have some First Amendment rights.

Dilemmas pointed up by Bellows's remarks, however, are not very different from what we experience today, though there is little threat of much government interference with programming. The attitude now prevailing in Congress is that programming is properly left to the market. If listeners are not happy with what they get, they have recourse to the on/off switch—a means of influencing programming that Herbert Hoover declared unacceptable—a means that also appears to be rarely used so far as evidence of much influence on program quality can be judged. Or maybe only the disgruntled so conclude.

The Public Interest Standard and the Constitution

The "public interest" standard as it was to be used by the two commissions was at best vague. It is, and was in 1927, established constitutional law that a legislative power may not be validly delegated in the absence of a standard for guidance in making decisions. The standard must be sufficiently definite to provide *meaningful*, not merely "apparent," guidance. Another purpose of the standard is clearly to notify those affected by the agency's decisions what is expected of them. Finally, the standard should afford reviewing bodies, like courts, the ability to determine if the standard has been properly applied in given cases. Was the "public interest" standard up to these constitutional requirements?

In 1930 the Radio Commission revoked the license of Nelson Brothers Bond and Mortgage Company. That company sued the commission in federal court claiming that by such action the commission violated the act. Nelson Brothers claimed they had been giving good service, and that the commission had misapplied the equalization features of its own formulas designed to satisfy the equality of area service command of the Davis Amendment. No constitutional issue was raised in the suit. The district court ruled against the plaintiff, a decision that the Supreme Court affirmed (289 U.S. 266, 1933). Because the licensee plaintiff had taken its license subject to a specific provision that gave the commission the right to revoke it at any time, adequacy of the service provided was irrelevant, the Supreme Court said. As to misapplication of the standard, the High Court analyzed the requirements of the Davis Amendment and could not fault the commission's interpretation. Further, the Court in effect read into the meaning of the more generally phrased "public interest" the specific requirements the commission had designed to meet Davis Amendment requirements. As thus employed by the commission, the "public interest" standard was found by the Court to be quite adequate. This decision appears to mean little more than that the loss by Nelson Brothers of its license was just one of the casualties of the effort to comply with the Davis Amendment, and thus to satisfy the "public convenience, interest, and necessity." In later cases the Supreme Court relied upon this decision as authority for the more sweeping proposition that the "public convenience, interest, and necessity" standard was sufficiently definite to meet the due process requirements of the Fifth Amendment.[2] Careful reading of the *Nelson Brothers* opinion makes such an interpretation difficult to defend.

Another problem with the public interest standard is its possible conflict with section 29 of the Radio Act (section 326 of the Communications Act), which denied the commission any power to censor program content.[3] It is sometimes said that section 29 built the First Amendment into that law, clearly an incorrect conclusion. If the First Amendment applies to broadcasting, there would have been no need for Congress to say anything in the statute. That aside, section 29 provisions applied solely to the Radio Commission (and the Communications Commission); its provisions were always subject to modification, even repeal, by Congress. In light of this "fragility" of its status, it could not be equivalent to a constitutional guarantee.

The question remains whether the commission's lack of power to censor or otherwise to control programming by virtue of section 29 affects its ability to force broadcasters to serve the public interest. Certainly program content is a matter of "public interest." Are these two sections of the act in conflict? In the matter of *Great Lakes Broadcasting Company*, a 1929 decision, the Radio Commission recognized that, under the act, only a limited number of those desiring to broadcast could do so, and gave notice that it expected programming to serve the interests of all listeners. Such programming, it said, should be well-rounded and should include

> entertainment, consisting of music of both classical and lighter grades, religion, education and instruction, important public events, discussions of public questions, weather, market reports, and news, and matters of interest to all members of the family. . . .
>
> In such a scheme there is no room for the operation of broadcasting stations exclusively by or in the private interests of individuals or

groups so far as the nature of the programs is concerned. There is not room in the broadcast band for every school of thought, religious, political, social, and economic, each to have its separate broadcasting stations, its mouthpiece in the ether. (Kahn 1978, 60)

This is certainly an echo of the position taken by the major broadcasters at Hoover's Radio Conferences, who labeled programming by "single-interest" licensees like the AFL-CIO "propaganda." It is also a clear commission statement asserting the commission's right to concern itself with program content. If needs of all types of listeners are to be met, but the number of available frequencies precludes separate providers for each such need, what is the solution? In the event, the ax fell on small stations— the so-called "propaganda" outlets.

Two such licensees fell before this commission analysis, judged to have acted contrary to the statutory standard. The first was station KFKB in Milford, Kansas, the license of which was held by "Dr." J. R. Brinkley. Brinkley's M.D. degree had been awarded by a school not accredited by the American Medical Association. His radio programming, on the air only a limited number of hours a day, consisted in large measure of advertisements and testimonials for his patent medicines. The doctor was also known for a surgical specialty he touted in which he purported to "restore" male potency by use of goat gonads. The surgery was performed at local Kansas hospitals. The station's signal was strong, the programs heard in many states. They seemed popular and worked to enlarge the number of pharmacists successfully dispensing Brinkley's patent medicines. The pharmacies enjoyed business in such medicines sufficient to make them enthusiastic supporters of Dr. Brinkley, and they expressed that support during the commission's renewal proceeding.

The station also carried some live music performances, but the Radio Commission concluded that KFKB programs were primarily devoted to the commercial purposes of promoting Brinkley's patent medicines and medical practice and, even though the station seemed popular, the commission declined renewal of KFKB's license on the grounds that it did not serve the public interest.

On appeal the station limited itself to arguing that the commission exceeded its authority in light of section 29. The court of appeals affirmed the commission decision (636 F.2d 432, 1931). Because broadcasting facilities are limited and broadcasting must be conducted in the "public interest," said the court, the commission is entitled to consider a licensee's prior programming in determining whether future programming is likely to meet that standard. Such a mode of proceeding, said the court, did not constitute censorship within the meaning of section 29. Whether such programming satisfied the public interest standard was a matter within the discretion of the commission. It was not open to second-guessing by courts unless the evidence demonstrated a clear abuse of discretion.

The second licensee denied renewal was Trinity Methodist Church South. Reverend "Bob Shuler, pastor of Trinity Church, used the station to present his strident views attacking the Roman Catholic Church, Jews, law enforcement officials of Los Angeles, and most politicians. In fact, few of prominence escaped his vitriol.

In the Trinity appeal (which came after the decision in Brinkley's case), Shuler argued that the nonrenewal not only violated section 29 of the Radio Act, but his First Amendment rights as well. Relying on its Brinkley decision, the court of appeals found no violation of section 29. As for the First Amendment, the court said that the purpose of that amendment was to prevent government interference with a publisher's right to publish or a speaker's right to say what he or she pleased; it did not protect publishers or speakers from consequences resulting from those choices. The court of appeals cited the recent Supreme Court decision in *Near v. Minnesota* (283 U.S. 691) as authority for this narrow Blackstone-like understanding of the reach of the amendment, even though the court in the *Near* case had concluded that "in the present case, we have no occasion to inquire as to the permissible [under the First Amendment] scope of subsequent punishment. . . . Liberty of the press historically considered and taken up by the Federal Constitution, has meant, principally *although not exclusively*, immunity from previous restraints or censorship" (283 U.S. 697, 716; emphasis added).

These remarks at least muddy the waters as to the Supreme Court's thinking and weaken reliance on *Near* by the court of appeals as support for its narrow definition of "freedom of the press." The Supreme Court, however, declined to review the *Trinity Methodist Church* case, and Shuler lost his broadcast license (47 F.2d 670, 1933).[4]

The Radio and Communications acts both had provisions limiting the term of a broadcast license and providing that the grant of a license did not give a licensee any right to contend, as against the government, that such license created any property interest in the licensee so far as the frequency licensed is concerned. The licensee agreed to such provision by its acceptance of the license. This eliminated any contention that broadcasters had a claim for what could be a heavy investment in the acquisition of broadcast equipment and possible construction of facilities, both in reliance on having been awarded a license. It did not, though, eliminate the political pressures created as a result of incurring such expenditures.

Although the commission was authorized to issue licenses only in a manner to serve the "public interest, convenience, and necessity," it was not *required* to issue any license at all. If it was not satisfied with an applicant, or applicants, in a particular case, it was free to withhold the license and wait for a better prospect.

These statutes provided for a good many technical matters, including reservation of frequencies for emergency uses such as coast guard, police, rescue work, ambulances, and assorted military and other governmental functions. Finally, they gave to the commission the power to make and enforce such rules and regulations with respect to broadcasting as should be required to carry out the purposes of the acts, all determined by the requirement that they serve the public interest.

In chapter 8 I examine actions of the Communications Commission in light of the foregoing inconsistencies in the course of administering the act. In the next chapter I examine two cases that raised First Amendment objections to government regulation of broadcasting and compare them with a case dealing with an attempt by Florida to impose some like regulations on newspapers.

Notes

1. Commissioners were to be appointed by the president for seven-year terms, subject to Senate confirmation. No more than four were to be from either of the two major parties, and the commission terms were staggered so that one was scheduled to expire each year. A good account of the organization and operation of the commission may be found in Hilliard 1991.

2. The court seems to so conclude in both *NBC v. FCC* 319 U.S. 190 (1943), and *Red Lion Broadcasting Co., Inc. v. FCC* 395 U.S. 367 (1969), two of the most defining cases in broadcast law.

3. That section provided in part, "Nothing in this chapter shall be understood or construed to give the Commission the power of censorship over radio communications or signals transmitted by any radio station, and no regulation or condition shall be promulgated or fixed by the Commission which shall interfere with the right of free speech by means of radio communication." Section 326 of the Communications Act is the same.

4. The court of appeals also anticipated some of the reasoning of the Supreme Court in the *Red Lion* case, noting that not everyone could be licensed to broadcast, weakening First Amendment claims relative to use of the electromagnetic spectrum.

CHAPTER 7

Media and the First Amendment

The First Amendment to the U.S. Constitution bars government infringement of freedom of speech or of the press. The impact of that rather clear-sounding formula has provoked a great deal of debate.

In 1798, during the presidency of John Adams and barely eight years after ratification of the Bill of Rights, the country was faced with questions as to the meaning of First Amendment guarantees. Fearful of influences arising from the French Revolution, Congress enacted the Alien and Sedition acts, which made it a crime to criticize the president and members of Congress in the performance of their duties. Although these statutes are widely thought today to have violated the First Amendment guarantees, their constitutionality was never questioned before the Supreme Court prior to their termination in 1801.

The Supreme Court was finally faced with a case requiring interpretation of the free speech guarantee in the early 20th century. In that case, *Patterson v. Colorado* 205 U.S. 454 (1907), Patterson, a newspaper editor, was held in contempt of the Colorado Supreme Court for publishing articles critical of political activities of that court's judges. The U.S. Supreme Court adopted the common law definition of "free press" set forth in Blackstone's 18th-century *Commentaries on the Common Law of England* as the meaning of those words in the Constitution, that is, that the amendment protected the press only from prior restraints. Because there was no prior restraint involved in Patterson's conviction, the court held that a newspaper editor could be punished for criticism adjudged to have disrupted judicial business.

During World War I the government was faced with resistance to prosecution of the war on the part of some groups who, though small in numbers, caused concern because of possible ties to Germany. Congress passed the Espionage and Sedition acts of 1918–19. A self-proclaimed socialist, Charles Schenck, was convicted of violating those acts by distributing antiwar leaflets urging members of the military to disobey their orders. Schenck appealed his conviction, claiming the statutes infringed the First Amendment. The Supreme Court affirmed the conviction, holding that such statutes were not unconstitutional when used by the government in face of clear and present danger threatening its ability to perform its legitimate governmental tasks. *Schenck v. U.S.* 249 U.S. 47 (1919) was a holding followed in later cases.

No case involving the press arose following the *Patterson* decision until 1931 when a district attorney in Minnesota obtained an injunction under a state statute preventing further publication by a weekly journal until it demonstrated to a court that it was no longer engaging in publication of libelous and scurrilous matter. In *Near v. Minnesota* 283 U.S. 691, the Supreme Court said that the statute that permitted such injunctions was unconstitutional. Whatever the reach of the First Amendment, said the Court, it clearly barred government from prior restraint of the press by preventing publication in advance.

Broadcasting: The First Case

Other cases were decided by the Supreme Court before 1943 involving speech issues, but none contributed much to resolution of issues presented to the Court in that year by the case of *NBC v. U.S.* 319 U.S. 190. The *NBC* case had been brought by the broadcast networks seeking an injunction to prevent the FCC from enforcing newly adopted chain-broadcasting rules.

The National Broadcasting Company was formed in 1926. A subsidiary of RCA, it operated the four radio stations licensed to that corporation. Its primary business, though, was production of programming to be supplied to affiliated, independently licensed radio stations around the country. NBC, which had the resources to produce programming of a high technical quality, was to radio what in many respects the Associated Press is to newspapers today. Because broadcasting was financed by advertising revenues, a group of broadcasters, able to assure an advertiser that its commercials would be heard by their combined audiences, could charge more for the commercials than could each singly, thus permitting a higher program production budget, yielding a higher profit margin for broadcasters, and providing the advertiser a lower charge per household reached. This was the service that NBC supplied to numerous licensees as well as to advertisers. Broadcasters so served were NBC affiliates, independents that chose to enter into a contract with NBC allowing them to identify themselves as NBC stations and to carry NBC-created programming. In 1928 CBS entered the field as a competitor of NBC and established its own network of affiliated stations.

In applying for an FCC license, a broadcaster, complying with agency requirements, would specify the type of programming intended to be carried. Under the Communications Act, those lucky enough to receive a broadcast license were not allowed to transfer that license without FCC approval. As the two networks grew, bringing a majority of stations into affiliation with one or the other, the FCC became concerned that independents were losing their autonomy in programming choices, and that affiliation might constitute a de facto assignment of the broadcast license without any FCC involvement. In 1938 FCC staff was instructed to study the developing situation.

The study's report led the commission to propose new chain-broadcast regulations that, among other things, limited network power to preempt prime time and banned restrictions on affiliates' rights to accept programming from other networks. The rules are set forth in the appendix to this chapter in summary form, as they appear in the *NBC* opinion. The rules were aimed at the independent broadcaster, not at the networks, because the commission had no authority over network activities beyond those in broadcasting by stations licensed to them.

The commission let it be known that failure to abide by the rules could present difficulties when independents sought renewal of their licenses. Prospective new licensees would be expected to declare their intent to follow these rules like any others.

The networks considered the rules to pose a serious threat to their operations and sued the commission in a federal district court in New York for an injunction to prevent the commission from enforcing them. In the suit, which became famous by reason of the ultimate Supreme Court decision, the networks urged three arguments in support of their case: (1) commission authority under the Communications Act was limited to prevention of signal interference; (2) if FCC authority exceeded that of a signal-interference traffic cop, such power was governed by a standard—public convenience, interest, and necessity—which is so vague as to be unconstitutional; and (3) the rules infringe on First Amendment rights of the network plaintiffs.

The district court in New York upheld the regulations and refused to issue the injunction. The case then went to the Supreme Court, which affirmed the district court's disposition of the case and dealt with the networks' contentions in the following manner. The requirement in the Communications Act that commission decisions had to serve the public interest indicated a discretion in the commission beyond that of simply being a traffic cop. Therefore, the FCC had greater authority under the act than that asserted by the networks. As for the vagueness of the standard, the Court said it was about as definite a standard as was possible given the complexity of the world of broadcasting. In support of this latter point, the court cited two cases, one of which was *Nelson Bros., Bond and Mortgage Co. v. FRC*. A careful reading of the *Nelson Brothers* case leads me to conclude the Court was not there required to consider validity of that standard, making the case questionable authority for use by the *NBC* court.

The fame of the *NBC* case rests mainly on the Court's treatment of the last contention made by the plaintiffs. As noted by Professors Thomas Krattenmaker and Lucas Powe (1994, 183), the position of the networks in presenting this constitutional issue was not one that tugged at the constitutional heartstrings of the justices. Exactly what speech interests the networks had in mind is not altogether clear; presumably it was their right to contract with broadcasters that would carry network programming over the airwaves licensed to these affiliates. The networks were very large and wealthy corporations. The affiliation contracts were for the most part nonnegotiable so far as the affiliate was concerned. In short, the case could be seen as an effort by these giant entities to vindicate their claimed First Amendment rights at the expense of similar rights of the weaker affiliates.

In an opinion written by Justice Felix Frankfurter, the Court dealt with the First Amendment contention as follows:

> We come, finally, to the First Amendment. The Regulations, even if valid in all other respects, must fall because they abridge, say the appellants, their right of free speech. If that be so, it would follow that every person whose application for a license to operate a station is denied by the Commission is thereby denied his constitutional right of free speech. Freedom of utterance is denied to many who wish to use the limited facilities of radio. Unlike other modes of expression, radio is inherently not available to all. That is its unique characteristic, and that is why, unlike other modes of expression, it is subject to governmental regulation. Because it cannot be used by all, some who wish to use it must be denied. . . . The question here is simply whether the Commission, by announc-

ing that it will refuse licenses to persons who engage in specified network practices. . . is thereby denying such persons the constitutional right of free speech. The right of free speech does not include, however, the right to use the facilities of radio without a license. The licensing system established by Congress in the Communications Act of 1934 was a proper exercise of its power over commerce. . . . Denial of a station license on that ground [public interest, convenience or necessity], if valid under the Act, is not a denial of free speech. (319 U.S. 190, 226)

The Court appears to be saying that if the chain broadcasting rules would violate the networks' First Amendment rights, it would follow that anyone denied a license to broadcast has also had his or her speech rights infringed. Frankfurter does not here address the preliminary question whether the real cause of the alleged infringement is the fact of signal interference or the license requirement. Rather, he assumes it is the latter, thus assuming the constitutional validity of the license requirement *sub silentio*. Is Frankfurter also saying that the power to deny any access to broadcasting includes the power to control everything said over the air?

Former Professor Harry Kalven of the University of Chicago Law School has expressed his perplexity as to what the Court meant: "Surely [NBC] was not arguing that radio could not be licensed at all because of the First Amendment. Yet that is the position that is being answered. Surely Justice Frankfurter is not suggesting that because facilities are limited, radio, unlike other modes of communication, is subject to unlimited government regulation. Yet that is what he has come close to saying" (Kalven 1967, 44).

The Court's opinion later asserts that "the licensing system . . . was a proper exercise of [Congress's] power over commerce." This echoes a statement in the *Nelson Brothers* case, an assertion by the Court that the licensing power was a proper one for Congress under the commerce clause (289 U.S. 266, 279). Such a conclusion was not a holding in the *Nelson Brothers* case because no contention had been made that Congress did *not* have the power to require a license to broadcast, putting the foregoing statement in the category of dictum. Simply echoing such dictum cannot be considered a serious effort to deal with a First Amendment challenge to such licensing power. Not only does it appear in the court's *NBC* opinion almost as an "aside," it is also extremely doubtful that the commerce clause alone could support such a conclusion. Print journalism is also in interstate commerce. It is a virtual certainty that government requirement of a license to publish a newspaper would not survive a First Amendment attack, notwithstanding the commerce clause.

The fourth sentence of the opinion states that "freedom of utterance is denied to many who wish to use the limited facilities of radio." Denied by whom? The government? Does this mean that as a result of the defining of available frequencies, not everyone may have a license under the Communications Act, or is it an assertion that because some radio users interfere with other radio users, the government may (or must) choose the winners and allocate the spectrum? Possibly a valid conclusion under the commerce clause, but First Amendment considerations are not even mentioned except to be simply ignored—with no reasons given.

Finally, we come to the flat assertion in the opinion that "the right of free speech does not include, however, the right to use the facilities of radio without a license." Any understanding of this opinion must start with examining the briefs of the parties to the case to determine exactly what issues they presented for the Court's decision. Such an examination reveals that neither network raised any question concerning constitutionality of the licensing scheme of the Communications Act. These plaintiffs virtually stipulated that the licensing scheme was valid, limiting their First Amendment argument to attacking commission authority under the act to impose the chain-broadcasting rules on stations licensed under the act.

In light of the parties' briefs, the last-quoted conclusion of the Court seems clearly to constitute no more than restatement by the Court of the virtual stipulation of the parties. That is also true of virtually all the Court's statements that might be read as upholding the constitutionality of licensing. That the Court would have made such an important decision as finding the licensing requirement constitutionally valid in the absence of argument in briefs, in the absence of a lower-court decision dealing with the question, and in the absence of any argument of counsel, is simply not credible.

Nonetheless, the outcome has generally been thought to be a holding that the requirement of a license to broadcast does not infringe the First Amendment. The FCC has been quite explicit in so viewing the case, concluding in its "1974 Fairness Report" (48 FCC 1, 4) that "in the case of National Broadcasting Co. v U.S. 319 U.S. 190 (1943), the Supreme Court concluded that because of the scarcity of available frequencies, the licensing system established by Congress did not violate the First Amendment."

Broadcasting: The Second Case

The next case, *Red Lion Broadcasting Co., Inc. v. FCC* 395 U.S. 367 (1969), considered the constitutionality of the fairness doctrine, which is discussed in detail in chapter 10. Briefly, the doctrine consists of a three-pronged policy developed by the FCC over many years. It required broadcasters to provide coverage of controversial issues in a balanced manner, the expression of other points of view, and time to any person criticized in the course of the broadcaster's coverage to reply to such criticism.

The *Red Lion* case arose out of the presidential election of 1964, during which one Fred Cook wrote a book critical of the Republican nominee, Barry Goldwater, titled *Goldwater, Extremist on the Right.* A Philadelphia radio station owned by Red Lion Broadcasting Company carried a review of Cook's book by the Reverend Billy Hargis, a conservative, who blasted the book, accusing Cook of being a liar and probably a communist. Cook asked Red Lion for an opportunity to reply to the review. The broadcaster refused, and Cook sought relief from the FCC, which ordered Red Lion to comply with Cook's demand. Claiming infringement of its First Amendment rights, Red Lion appealed the FCC order to the D.C. court of appeals, which ruled for the FCC in a decision then reviewed by the Supreme Court. That Court upheld the constitutionality of the doctrine in an opinion also considered by many as holding that the *licensing* requirement under the Communications Act does not infringe the First Amendment. But in *Red Lion*, as in *NBC*, no party attacked the constitutionality of licensing. The briefs of all parties clearly demonstrate that they accepted the act's requirement of a license to broadcast as valid; it was not impugned as violative of the First Amendment.

Language in the Court's opinion, ambiguous like that in *NBC*, provides some support for those believing the constitutional issue of licensing to have been addressed. For example, in one place the Court said:

> It would be strange if the First Amendment, aimed at protecting and furthering communications, prevented the Government from making radio communication possible by requiring licenses to broadcast and by limiting the number of licenses so as not to overcrowd the spectrum.
>
> This has been the consistent view of the Court. Congress unquestionably has the power to grant and deny licenses and to eliminate existing stations. *FRC v Nelson Bros. Bond & Mortgage Company* 289 U.S. 266 (1933). No one has a First Amendment right to a license or to mo-

nopolize a radio frequency; to deny a station license because "the public interest" requires it "is not a denial of free speech." *National Broadcasting Co. v United States,* 319 U.S. 190, 227 (1943). [395 U.S. 367, 389]

The foregoing reliance on the earlier cases presents problems. The *Nelson Brothers* case, also cited by the Court in its *NBC* decision, does not even mention the First Amendment. In that case the Court upheld commission power to revoke the license of Nelson Brothers, a right the commission had reserved in issuing the license in the first place. Nelson Brothers, having accepted the license in that form many years before, would have had a tough time arguing that revocation violated its rights. In fact, it did not so argue; its contentions were limited to urging that the commission misapplied the 1928 Davis Amendment to the Radio Act, as well as to the commission's own standards, in the process of determining to revoke the Nelson Brothers license. The only assist to the *Red Lion* opinion is the statement that enactment was within congressional power under the Commerce Clause, a statement apparently also relied on in the *NBC* opinion but providing no real support for the decision in either *NBC* or *Red Lion.*

The earlier analysis of the *NBC* case demonstrates the difficulties of the *Red Lion* Court's reliance on the *NBC* decision. Encapsulating that difficulty, the First Amendment question alleged by the *Red Lion* Court to have been decided by the Court in *NBC* wasn't even litigated in that case.

The ground for the Supreme Court's ruling in *Red Lion* upholding the constitutionality of the fairness doctrine is, I believe, the fact that the station was a licensee of the federal government by virtue of the Communications Act, a necessity that the licensee did not question. As a licensee, Red Lion enjoyed the privileged status of being one of the would-be broadcasters lucky enough to win such a privilege within the framework of the federal scheme. Such licenses were "scarce," a consequence as much of the requirement of a license as of the physical nature of the spectrum. Therefore, the government had the right to impose "trusteeship" obligations on those lucky few receiving such licenses, obligations requiring them to "serve the public interest"—obligations the imposition of which did not violate their First Amendment rights.

Some might wonder why broadcasters did not argue the constitutional question. The likely answer is that they had no wish to see the licensing system end. That system had rescued the broadcasting industry from chaos in the 1920s and ensured each broadcaster a monopoly in its frequency, protected by government from signal interference, a result for which they had lobbied. Its end would probably result in chaos once more.

Broadcasters probably concluded that an attempt to kill the goose that laid the golden egg would not be in their interest.

Newspapers

Five years following the *Red Lion* decision, the Court decided *Miami Herald v. Tornillo* 418 U.S. 241 (1974). That case presented the Court with the question of the constitutionality under the First Amendment of a state law requiring newspapers that criticized candidates for political office to make space available in the paper for the candidate so criticized to reply at no charge. Tornillo, a candidate for a seat in the Florida state legislature, was criticized by the *Herald*. He demanded a right to reply pursuant to the state statute. The newspaper resisted, citing its First Amendment rights. The Florida Supreme Court upheld the statute, ruling against the newspaper. In language reminiscent of the *Red Lion* opinion, the Florida court reasoned that the statute served to enhance First Amendment values by encouraging more information to be supplied the electorate rather than less. The U.S. Supreme Court did not see it that way. In a unanimous opinion it reversed the Florida decision, holding the statute to be a clear interference with the journal's editorial judgment in violation of its First Amendment rights. It opined that the Florida statute would operate to chill the open and robust debate, preservation of which is a purpose of the First Amendment, and which is so important to a free society.

Critics of government regulation of broadcasting consider the two broadcast decisions previously discussed to be in irreconcilable conflict with the decision in *Miami Herald v. Tornillo*. They apparently believe that the Court upheld government regulation of broadcasting, including the license requirement, because of the "scarcity" of radio frequencies and belittle that rationale on the ground that *all resources are scarce*. Pointing out that newsprint, printer's ink, and other items used in publishing a newspaper are also scarce, such critics conclude, in the words of Robert Bork: "There may be ways to reconcile *Red Lion* and *Tornillo* but the 'scarcity' of broadcast frequencies does not appear capable of doing so" *Telecommunications Research and Action Center v. FCC* 801 F.2d 501, 509 (D.C. Cir. 1986).

I contend that this critique of the holdings in the two broadcast cases rests on an erroneous reading of those cases. Those holdings are grounded in the fact that the broadcasters are *licensees* of the federal government, not on the scarcity of frequencies. Broadcasters in both cases had accepted their licensee status, virtually stipulating that such licensing was necessary to overcome interference problems resulting from the scarcity of broadcast frequencies. The Court accepted this account of the origins of the licensing requirement, an account described in all briefs. With no reason to question that account, the Court proceeded to consider the validity of the chain-broadcasting rules in *NBC* and the fairness doctrine in *Red Lion*.

Another distinction between *Tornillo* and the two broadcast cases, mentioned neither in the *Tornillo* opinion nor elsewhere so far as I am aware, is that the broadcast cases, dealing with a federal statute, applied to the nation as a whole. The *Miami Herald* case dealt only with a Florida law. The holdings in *NBC* and *Red Lion* applied uniformly throughout the country. Upholding the Florida statute could have led to a multitude of differing state laws affecting newspaper speech in many ways, probably an undesirable result.[1]

Although no court has considered whether "scarcity" could justify requiring a license to broadcast, in my opinion that characteristic, in combination with concerns of monopolization of the medium, can provide such a justification, a view developed in more detail in chapter 13.

Notes

1. The court opinion does refer to contentions made by Tornillo's counsel that various Supreme Court justices had, in prior cases, suggested a need for state laws to overcome some of the deficiencies of our current press.

APPENDIX

Chain-Broadcasting Rules as Summarized in *NBC v. U.S.*

1. No license shall be granted to a standard broadcast station having any contract, arrangement, or understanding with a network organization under which the station is prevented or hindered from, or penalized for, broadcasting the programs of any other network organization.

2. No license shall be granted to a standard broadcast station having any contract, etc., with a network organization which prevents or hinders another station serving substantially the same area from broadcasting the network's programs not taken by the former station, or which prevents or hinders another station serving a substantially different area from broadcasting any program of the network organization; but not prohibiting any contract between a station and a network organization pursuant to which the station is granted the first call in its primary service area upon the programs of the network organization.

3. No license shall be granted to a standard broadcast station having any contract, etc., with a network organization which provides for the affiliation of the station with the network organization for a period longer than two years.

4. No license shall be granted to a standard broadcast station which options for network programs any time subject to call on less than 56 days' notice, or more time than a total of three hours within each of four segments of the broadcast day, as described in the regulation, and that such options may not be exclusive as against other network organizations and may not prevent or hinder the station from optioning any or all of the time covered by the option, or other time, to other network organizations.

5. No license shall be granted to a standard broadcast station having any contract, etc., with a network organization which (a), with respect to programs offered pursuant to an affiliation contract, prevents or hinders the station from rejecting or refusing network programs which the station reasonably believes to be unsatisfactory or unsuitable; or which (b), with respect to network programs so offered or already contracted for, prevents the station from rejecting or refusing any program which, in its opinion, is contrary to the public interest, or from substituting a program of outstanding local or national importance.

6. No license shall be issued to a network organization, or to any person directly or indirectly controlled by or under common control with a

network organization, for more than one standard broadcast station where one of the stations covers substantially the service area of the other station, or for any standard broadcast station in any locality where the existing standard broadcast stations are so few or of such unequal desirability (in terms of coverage, power, frequency, or other related matters) that competition would be substantially restrained by such licensing.

7. No license shall be granted to a standard broadcast station having a contract, etc., with a network organization under which the station is prevented or hindered from, or penalized for, fixing or altering its rates for the sale of broadcast time for other than the network's programs.

CHAPTER 8

The Industry's Regulators

The Federal Communications Act of 1934 was little changed from the Radio Act it replaced. The major differences were placing interstate telephone operations and their rates under the regulatory jurisdiction of the commission, renaming the commission the "Communications Commission," and making that body a permanent agency. This chapter examines in some detail how the commission used its authority through the years with respect to broadcasting.

The actions of the Radio Commission under the Radio Act had for the most part favored the interests of the large commercial broadcasters owned or affiliated with the major networks, NBC and CBS. Together the two networks also owned the 10 or 15 most important stations in the country. RCA and its parents (and members of the RCA cartel), AT&T, Westinghouse, and General Electric, had been the most influential voices heard in the government's development of the regulatory climate and the allocation of frequencies. Smaller, noncommercial stations such as those of colleges, universities, churches, unions, and assorted civic groups had been assigned less desirable frequencies on the spectrum, and even those lesser positions were gradually giving way to the surge of commercial broadcasting. The least desirable of all went to the amateurs. It was this situation that the newly created Federal Communications Commission inherited in 1934.

Historians are traditionally preoccupied with whether things might have been different from what they turned out to be. This ailment is simply another manifestation of the old argument about freedom versus determinism. In the eyes of many, broadcasting had become the handmaiden of American corporations and the advertising medium of choice for creating market demand where none would otherwise exist. Was this an "inevitable" outcome, or might noncommercial interests have succeeded in retaining at least a significant piece of the action? In his *Telecommunications, Mass Media, and Democracy,* Robert W. McChesney observes that recent efforts to reexamine broadcasting's origins in the United States have tended to conclude that by 1922 the shape of American broadcasting as the fiefdom of large corporations had been firmly established. On page 4 of his book he cites Susan J. Douglas's *Inventing American Broadcasting, 1899–1922* as illustrative of his contention. McChesney himself rejects such a deterministic view. Of course the bona fides of his book to some extent depend on such a rejection because his subject is the struggle in the early 1930s to restore to the electromagnetic spectrum the active involvement of educational and other noncommercial interests. McChesney has to believe the effort to do so was not foredoomed to failure.

It seems overdrawn to say that Douglas, had she considered the matter, would have concluded that the efforts described by McChesney didn't stand a chance. More likely, the outcome would not have surprised her, even if she didn't view it as inevitable. Perhaps this is of academic interest only. After all, neither Douglas nor McChesney was old enough to be a participant in the events they discuss. Returning to the Communications Act, the numerous commissioners operating through the years under its authority seem to have accepted the shape of the media as received from the Radio Commission and not generally to have adopted policies calculated to "rock the boat." Persons appointed to the commission have usually had prior experience in government and were often attorneys by training. Some came from the broadcasting world, and a majority, on leaving the commission, went to good-paying jobs in the industry they had been regulating. One might conclude that commissioners came and went, but the interests of commercial broadcasters held a steady course.

The FCC has always had a staff. Many of its members have been, and are today, engineers knowledgeable with respect to the electromagnetic spectrum. Their training not unnaturally has led them to carry on the tradition begun by the Radio Commission, which seemed grounded in an engineering understanding of the problems presented by broadcasting, an understanding often based on the idea that the "public interest" was satisfied by elimination of signal interference.

There have been exceptions to this general trend. In 1939 President Roosevelt named James Lawrence Fly to be chairman of the commission. Fly took an activist position with respect to the obligations of both commission and broadcasters under the Communications Act. It was during the Fly period that the commission issued its famous *Mayflower* decision

(8 FCC 339, 1941), which required licensees to be impartial in their coverage of issues of public concern. The commission described one station in the case, whose license renewal was being considered, as having "broadcast so-called editorials from time to time urging the election of various candidates for political office or supporting one side or another of various questions in public controversy. . . . No pretense was made at objective, impartial reporting. It is clear—indeed the station seems to have taken pride in the fact—that the purpose of these editorials was to win public support for some person or view favored by those in control of the station."

In this echo of the early contention of the large broadcasters that small licensees, like the AFL-CIO, were "propagandists," we now find regulatory activists accusing the large and network-affiliated stations of themselves behaving like "propagandists"—clearly not up to the "public interest" standard. The commission decided the public interest standard required that licensees desist from editorializing.

From this decision grew the fairness doctrine—not full-blown, but developed over years. The commission first reversed itself as to station editorializing. Rather than forbid the practice, it concluded stations could editorialize but must give equal coverage to all aspects of the matters at issue. This led to commission policy requiring licensees to cover issues of public concern, exploring all sides of the issues in an impartial manner. In its final form the doctrine required broadcast licensees to cover controversial issues; to cover all sides of such issues fairly; and to afford persons criticized in the course of such coverage an opportunity to reply, free of charge and under conditions substantially like those under which the criticism had been aired.

The fairness doctrine thereafter governed broadcasting without being seriously questioned until 1964 when Red Lion Broadcasting Company questioned its constitutionality. As discussed in chapter 7, the Supreme Court upheld the doctrine's validity in the lawsuit brought by Red Lion, and the doctrine continued in effect until 1987, when the commission decided that it no longer served the public interest (if it ever had) and that it infringed First Amendment rights of broadcasters. This commission decision is examined in more detail in chapter 11.

In another noteworthy action during the tenure of Commissioner Fly, the commission undertook a study of network influence over programming of independents. This led to FCC adoption (under Fly's successor, Paul A. Porter) of the so-called chain-broadcasting rules.

"Chain broadcasting" was broadcasting the same programming by a number of stations all affiliated with the same network. The network supplied affiliated stations with programs of high technical quality and proved popularity, and at a cost far lower than those independents could generally afford on their own. The arrangement also provided the network with a wide program—exposure that it could sell to prospective advertisers, while the affiliates benefited from enhanced advertising revenue they could charge for such proved and popular programs.

The contract document that governed the network/independent affiliation was in a "form" devised by the networks and subject to little if any negotiation. Provisions in such contracts that the commission found objectionable included denying the affiliate any right to take programs from another network, network rights to preempt prime time hours, and some network control over local advertising rates. The commission position was that licensees under the Communications Act are responsible for their programming, a responsibility requiring licensees to use their own judgment in program choice. In the commission's view the affiliation agreements required the independents to surrender important program decisions to the networks; in effect, this was an "assignment" of an important decision-making responsibility.

Because the commission had no authority over the networks (except with respect to the stations they operated), the chain-broadcasting rules (summarized in the appendix to chapter 7), intended to break much of the network hold over independents, were directed at the independent affiliates. The commission was telling the independents that if they entered into network contracts that contained the objectionable provisions, their license might not be renewed. The networks brought suit in an effort to prevent the rules from being enforced, claiming the FCC had no authority to issue them. The decision of the Supreme Court in *NBC v. U.S.* in which it upheld the rules, is discussed in chapter 7.

Years after the *NBC* case was decided, Newton Minow (having himself been an FCC chairman during the Kennedy administration) wrote that adoption of the chain-broadcasting rules was for the purpose of giving "the radio and network affiliates greater discretion in their local program schedules, . . . foster[ing] more local service and mak[ing] American broadcasting more competitive" (Minow and LaMay 1995, 88).

From its beginning in 1934 the commission had received evidence of public dissatisfaction with broadcast content. Letters showed unhappiness with program quality, with allegedly false and misleading advertising, with suggestive matter bordering on the "obscene," and with failure to deal with important issues, local or national. Commissioners had long felt ambivalent about imposing program standards or requirements on licensees. Reluctant to interfere with "free speech" and mindful of section 29, as well as difficulties in even defining appropriate program-content standards on such a vast scale, the commission usually relied on persuasion and jaw-boning as its primary weapons for influencing quality. Both the fairness doctrine and the chain-broadcasting rules were significant departures from this general course.

In spite of NBC's defeat in the effort to limit commission power, that network's parent, RCA, was a dominant force in both broadcasting and the market for radio hardware. It also seemed to exercise much control over FCC decisions.

> Certainly no communications executive worked more assiduously than David Sarnoff to cultivate a cordial spirit of cooperation between RCA and members of the commission. As most of the commissioners had been lawyers or government bureaucrats, devoid of the technical competence to understand the industry they were charged to regulate, Sarnoff found it relatively easy to bend their thinking to his will. When he or other RCA executives testified to the commission, they did so with firm authority, often backed by data produced by a phalanx of RCA engineers. Surely, Sarnoff would subtly assert, the largest communication corporation in the world had the ability to understand the increasingly sophisticated engineering concepts underlying radio better than any small company, individual entrepreneur, or inventor. Surely it was operating in the national interest. (Lewis 1991, 301–2)

RCA's influence over FCC actions was a tribute to the engineering expertise of RCA's staff and to the skills of David Sarnoff in bringing his own extensive knowledge to bear in persuading the less-well-informed commissioners of the rightness of the course espoused by RCA. Even so, the RCA team did not always prevail, as we have seen.

The commission chairman when the chain-broadcasting rules were issued was Paul A. Porter, Lawrence Fly's successor. An attorney who had once been a newspaper reporter, Porter had also served as Washington counsel for CBS for five years. When appointed by Franklin Roosevelt, Porter possessed experience that made him well-schooled in the ways of the FCC and the world of broadcasting. The most significant action of the commission under Porter, aside from promulgation of the chain-broadcasting rules, was the attempt to prescribe in greater detail those FCC policies designed to satisfy the public interest standard. In this way not only would the commission be given extended guidance in granting new station licenses and in considering license renewal, but the licensees would be made aware of the standards they would have to meet, thus avoiding facing the commission on an ad hoc basis. These policies were set forth in *Public Service Responsibility of Broadcast Licensees*, commonly called the Blue Book because of the color of its cover.

The Blue Book was intended to be useful to broadcasters as a compilation of requirements resulting from prior FCC and court decisions, alerting licensees and potential licensees of commission standards and ensuring consistency in FCC proceedings. The Blue Book called for licensees (a) to provide some sustained (not sponsor-financed) programs, (b) to carry some programs utilizing local talent, (c) to provide some programming dealing with important public issues, and (d) to minimize commercial advertising.

The concepts were neither radical nor particularly new, but broadcasters were enraged when they learned of the book's contents. Soon to follow, and equally shrill, was the response from the broadcasters' friends (and there were many) in Congress.

The commission did not repudiate the Blue Book but, in another instance of benign neglect, simply failed to enforce it. The FCC never denied renewal of any license (much less a revoked one) because of alleged failure to meet Blue Book standards. Several times licensees, although receiving license renewal, were admonished for failing to live up to the standards, but "disciplinary" action did not go beyond admonition. The Blue Book simply sank into obscurity from disuse. Decisions in license renewal proceedings continued, as in the past, to be more or less based on ad hoc determinations.

During Porter's venue the commission also adopted the frequency allocations for FM and television as discussed in chapter 9. Such allocations favored TV over radio apparently as a consequence of the persuasiveness of polished presentations put together by RCA and CBS addressing arguments that radio should be the major user of FM, a cause led by the inventor of FM, Howard Armstrong.

From time to time, and with occasional modifications, other policies adopted by the commission specifically intended to foster broadcasting in the public interest included:

1. Ascertainment requirements: These took several forms, all intended to require broadcasters to make some attempt to determine listening needs of the proposed target audience and to indicate means by which the license applicant proposed to meet such needs.

2. Ownership concentration: The commission believed that programming diversification was necessary to maximize public service. It also believed that the greater the number of independent licensee broadcasters, the greater the chances for achieving the desired diversity; the more concentrated ownership of stations, the poorer such chances. It therefore adopted rules restricting common ownership of broadcast stations, and of broadcast stations in combination with other media forms.

3. Localism: The commission considered that stations should serve the needs of local audiences. This policy was implemented by favoring license applicants who were familiar with, or residents of, the local service area and who were knowledgeable about and would cover locally important problems.

With the end of the Truman administration and Eisenhower's accession to the presidency, years of Democratic domination of the federal government ended. This also brought about change in policies of the Communications Commission, though such changes were often more cosmetic than real.

John Doerfer was named by Eisenhower the new chairman of the commission, and regulation of broadcasting during his tenure was executed with a light touch. Citing European governmental control over broadcast content as a horrible example, Doerfer praised the American approach under which the people determined the programming. He thought the FCC should have little power in that arena; in any case, he opposed attempts to prescribe standards to which programming should adhere.

The 1950s are often referred to as the golden age of television. Many excellent programs, including outstanding dramatic presentations, were enjoyed by wide segments of the TV audience. This pattern was not to last. Unfortunately for John Doerfer, the TV quiz scandals broke during his term. The highly popular *Twenty-One* was revealed to have been "fixed." When a well-known contestant, Charles Van Doren, who taught English literature at Columbia University, was faced with rumors of cheating, he made a public confession, thus ending his career in education. He had been fed answers in order to assure his continuing dominance of the show. The cheating was a public relations ploy prompted by Van Doren's popularity with the viewers, who stayed with the program to cheer on the likable, charismatic, and apparently brainy Van Doren. Growing audiences made sponsors happy, creating greater demand for advertising placement and increasing the amounts that could be charged for such commercials. That made both producers and networks happy.

Another show, *The $64,000 Question,* also came under suspicion. Apparently nothing was proved , but the quiz show format had been badly damaged, and the FCC's role as watchdog suffered along with it. Simultaneously Dr. Bernard Schwartz, counsel to the House Committee on Legislative Oversight, began investigations into the roots of these TV scandals, which led him also to look into charges of alleged misconduct on the part of federal agency officials. He targeted the FCC—Doerfer in particular.

Without notice to Doerfer, Schwartz leaked information charging him with official misconduct, undue fraternization with broadcasters, and defrauding of the government. Doerfer was subjected to relentless questioning by Schwartz before the House Committee. Incensed, the FCC chairman mounted a stout defense. Schwartz charged Doerfer with accepting payment for costs of travel for public appearances—travel for which he was also reimbursed by the government—and having too-close social relationships with owners of stations subject to FCC regulation. An angry Doerfer replied that he saw nothing wrong with his honorarium including expenses for which his job entitled him. As to the charge of being too cozy with regulatees, Doerfer responded:

> Probably 10% of [a commissioner's] work involves litigated matters. In such cases, we sit as judges. When I sit as a judge, I act as a judge. When I have matters for decision between litigants, I do not discuss these matters with either side, or, for that matter, with anyone. But when I am a legislator looking for information to solve some of the great problems confronting communications in the country, I will talk to anyone . . . in my office . . . on the steps of the Capitol or . . . at any public restaurant. (Emery 1971, 470)

Notwithstanding Doerfer's stated determination to ride out the controversy, the investigation took its toll and weakened his effectiveness. Within a few months he resigned from the commission.

There can be little doubt that both the kinds of activities commissioners are required to pursue and the political nature of their appointment contribute to at least an appearance of conflict of interest. Commissioners are required by the Communications Act both to make rules and to act as judges. Such a dual role would be difficult for anyone and is one of the primary reasons American government was founded upon the concept of the "separation of powers." But Congress has been unwilling to recognize its responsibility for the Communications Act provisions that place commissioners in such a position. Rather, some members of Congress appear to like having targets at which to shoot; as a result there is constant sniping, largely for political advantage, at commission decisions. This state of affairs is one consequence of our national failure to formulate an internally consistent role for government with respect to broadcasting, whether that role is to see that licensees serve the public interest, or to protect licensees from signal interference in order to safeguard the investment of the station's owners. When both are options, conflicts are inevitable. Occupants of FCC chairs usually find a path to financial security—after leaving the commission, of course—but the job can also become an uncomfortable "hot seat."

Another Eisenhower appointee, Richard Mack, was indicted for taking a bribe for his vote in a commission proceeding; he resigned about a year before Doerfer. These were probably the worst years for the commission as far as accusations of official misconduct are concerned.

In writing the Communications Act, Congress did not neglect the role of broadcasting in elections. Enforcement of relevant provisions was left primarily to the commission. One section (315) requires broadcasters to make time available for opposing candidates for public office when one candidate for that office has appeared on a station. This is the so-called "equal time" rule. It comes into play *only* after a broadcaster has allowed one candidate for office to appear on the station. The broadcaster then must make available to opponents time slots of comparable exposure and duration. The station is required to charge all subsequent candidates the same amount the first has been charged, or to offer airtime free of charge if the first candidate's time was free. The obligations of this section apply to all political candidacies—national, state, or local.

There are exceptions under section 315 with respect to some station coverage. Programs featuring the candidate at a bona fide news conference or other legitimate newsworthy event, as opposed to an election campaign appearance, do not trigger equal time rights for opponents. If the facts involve a close call, the FCC can make the final decision.

Another section of the act deals with commission power to revoke broadcast licenses (section 312). One ground for revocation is "continuous or willful" refusal to make reasonable amounts of broadcast time available for purchase by candidates for federal office once the election campaign has begun. The section further provides limits on the amounts that can be charged for such time, that is, the lowest applicable station rates. The requirement is complicated and rarely the subject of litigation. For example, the definitions of "willful" or "unreasonable," not to mention "adequate" amounts of time, are difficult to establish. One thing the courts have decided is that the commission may decide whether or not a campaign has begun. A broadcaster licensee's conclusion can be overruled.

In 1970 Nicholas Zapple, as counsel to the Senate Communications Subcommittee, inquired of the commission whether the fairness doctrine plays a role when a spokesperson for a candidate (as opposed to the candidate him- or herself) makes an appearance on a station in support of the candidate. The commission responded that the doctrine would require that a broadcaster afford equal time and comparable conditions to a spokesperson for other candidates for that office. This combination of the equal time rule with elements of the fairness doctrine became known as the Zapple doctrine.

Virtually all commission policies intended to serve the public interest were also originally intended to increase diversification of programming. Two other FCC moves in that direction have proved highly controversial. In 1978, taking note that most of its licensees were white males, the commission proceeded to adopt a so-called female preference policy. If more than one applicant sought a license, one being female, and competitive evaluation produced a draw, the female was to receive the license. Constitutionality of the policy was attacked as denying to males equal protection of the laws guaranteed under the Fifth Amendment. After a bizarre series of events, the court of appeals agreed with the attack against the policy. Programming, said the court, is primarily market driven; therefore, there is no substantial reason to believe that program diversification will be affected by the gender of the licensee. Consequently, the commission has no power under the act to undertake what appears to be social engineering with no relationship to its statutory duties (*Lamprecht v. FCC* 958 F.2d 382, 1992).

The second policy, or set of policies, resulted from a concern that there are too few minority license applicants, not to mention licensees. The commission thus sought to increase the number of broadcasters falling within the "minority" classification as defined by the policy. As with the example concerning the female preference policy, wherein all applicants were otherwise equal and one was a minority applicant, the license was again awarded to the minority applicant. Two additional policies were also adopted to further minority licensing, one having to do with sales to minorities of station licenses in danger of revocation, the other concerning the postponement of tax-realization. Neither of these, however, has had much impact. In fact, over a nine-year period all three of these minority policies increased the number of minority station owners by about .04 percent.

The minority preference policy did, though, affect individual applicants. One who lost to a group classified as Hispanic (a classification
within the definition of a minority) appealed the award on the same
grounds that the female preference policy had been attacked. Timing was
everything. A peculiar combination of circumstances brought this case to
the Supreme Court several years before the female preference policy was to
meet its end in the court of appeals. In *Metro Broadcasting v. FCC* 497 U.S.
547 (1990), the Supreme Court decided that the policy was *not* unconstitutional. Radio and television programming are not, said the court,
"wholly market driven"; therefore, the commission's conclusion that minority ownership of stations could contribute to program diversity was not
unreasonable. On the grounds of remedying past discrimination and
achieving program diversification, the policy survived constitutional attack.

The refusal of the Supreme Court to review the later court of appeals
decision striking down the female preference policy left the anomalous situation under which one policy was unconstitutional because programming
is *almost wholly* market driven, while an analogous policy is valid because
programming is not *entirely* market driven. Neither court quantified the
extent by which programming is *not* market driven. If that factor were
given the value of x and was not otherwise numerically calculable, it would
follow that the same reasoning produced apparently inconsistent results.

Even as the Communications Act on the one hand requires that
broadcasting serve the public interest, and on the other hand repudiates
any interference with program content by a government power, individual
commission members have through the years emphasized either the importance of serving the public, or, alternatively, the free speech rights of
broadcasters. The commission rarely, if ever, has demonstrated unanimity
regarding which interest should dominate. Many commentators conclude
from this ambivalence that overall commission regulation of broadcasting
has been conducted with a light hand. This is probably a valid conclusion,
though in revealing the philosophical bent of individual members of the
commission, it is misleading.

With the exception of the deregulatory activities of the FCC between
1980 and 1992 and, some might say, adoption of the fairness doctrine and
the Blue Book in the decade of the 1940s, FCC members have rarely been
sufficiently of one mind to give total support to one interest or the other.
More often than not, commission membership has been thought friendly
to the interests of broadcasters. The deregulatory movement that started in
the 1970s and continues to this day certainly has been. This makes quite

credible the conclusion that those who were to be competitively selected by the commission to broadcast, and who were subject to commission overview to ensure service of the public interest, ended up being considered "clients" whose interests were protected by the commission.

John Kennedy's presidency seemed slated to be different. In the end, though, the differences turned out to be cosmetic. Some fireworks were provided in a speech delivered by Newton Minow, the new president's choice to chair the commission. Characterizing television programming as a "vast wasteland," Minow accused the industry of not living up to its public obligations. No commission action during Minow's roughly 18-month tenure disturbed broadcasters nearly as much as this famous speech. Upon Minow's departure, Kennedy named Emil Henry his successor. Henry was of the same stripe as Minow (though not given to making disturbing speeches) and strove to reduce the influence of the networks over primetime programming. Perhaps in partial implementation of that effort the commission in 1964 acted to strengthen limitations on the number of major-market TV stations that could be under common ownership. Such constraint usually took the form of altering the allowed percentage of total viewing audience served by stations under common ownership. In the same year the commission also issued an extensive policy statement, "Applicability of the Fairness Doctrine in the Handling of Controversial Issues of Public Importance." This report, probably conceived during Minow's tenure, set forth in considerable detail the requirements of the fairness doctrine and the importance the commission attached to its enforcement.

Two further appointments stirred the broadcast world to the boiling point. Kenneth A. Cox, appointed by Kennedy, and Nicholas Johnson, appointed by President Johnson, were both young liberals considered "fire eaters." Strong believers in the principle that broadcasting should serve the public, they often expressed considerable umbrage at the state of American broadcasting and were attacked in *Broadcasting,* semiofficial journal of the broadcasting industry.

So far as provocation of editorial pyrotechnics is concerned, these three men (Henry being the nonvocal one) probably represented a high point in FCC activism, eliciting strong industry reaction.

> In general, the reasons for the Cox and Johnson castigations by *Broadcasting* and some other trade journals are much the same as they were for the attacks by these publications against former FCC "activist" members Walker, Durr, Fly, [and] Minow . . . —their insistence that the airways are public property, that broadcast monopolies must be strictly con-

trolled and competition preserved, that licensees are obligated to provide programs in terms of community needs and interests, be fair in the presentation of points of view on controversial issues of public importance, and their belief that the commission has the authority and duty to set minimum program standards and require stations to live up to them, all of which, in referring to [Nicholas] Johnson, *Broadcasting* has described as "espousal of rigid control of programs and business affairs—a sort of socialism." (Emery 1971, 488–89)

Emil Henry left the commission in 1966, and President Johnson appointed Rosel H. Hyde, then a member of the commission, to be its new chairman. First appointed to the FCC by President Eisenhower, Hyde served on the commission longer than any other person. He seemed an odd choice for Lyndon Johnson following appointment of Nicholas Johnson, because Hyde was considered the broadcaster's friend. He generally came down on the side of broadcasters' "rights" as opposed to conflicting rights of an amorphous group identified as "listeners." In harmony with his concern for broadcasters' problems, the commission under Hyde undertook to regulate CATV operations, which were considered to collide with interests of FCC licensees. This led to the Supreme Court's 1968 decision in *Southwestern Cable Co. v. FCC* (392 U.S. 157), which upheld a loosely defined commission jurisdiction over cable operations.

Hyde left the commission for good in 1969. One observer of the FCC described the decade then ending:

> At no previous time in the history of the Commission were the ideological conflicts among its members sharper and more pronounced. Intensifying these FCC rifts was the almost constant surveillance and intermeddling of Congress, aided and abetted by the critical clamor and outcries of the broadcast industry, the cable operators, the trade press, and other special interests, not to mention an aroused and sometimes hostile public. The FCC offices were even picketed by a disgruntled group led by a Reverend Carl McIntire, protesting an FCC requirement that he follow the "fairness doctrine" with respect to broadcasting of programs dealing with controversial issues of public importance. (Emery 1971, 487)

With the election of Richard Nixon, the FCC climate once again became generally favorable to broadcasters. Dean Burch, Hyde's successor as chairman, adopted a hands-off approach to broadcast regulation. He served until 1974, when Nixon named Richard E. Wiley to succeeed him. Like Burch (and Hyde), Wiley was considered an ally of broadcasters and consistently resisted attempts at increasing government regulation of the medium. He thought that the license term of three years was too short. He contended that no one should have to try to function in an atmosphere of constant upheaval engendered by so short a term, particularly faced with the unpredictable fluctuations in commission policy. He worked to simplify license renewal procedures and to increase the license term to five years.

One of Wiley's co-commissioners, Abbott Washburn (also appointed by Nixon) applied himself to reducing the commission-specified dimensions for satellite dishes because their large required size discouraged their use. His efforts bore fruit when such dimensions were reduced in 1975. Washburn attributed the success of pay TV, HBO, and Showtime to that change, which was followed by a very large increase in the number of satellite receivers. Washburn also encouraged FCC licensing of low-power television stations (LPT). A proponent of noncommercial TV operations, Washburn sought to encourage license applications of that kind by placing restrictions on multiple TV station ownership. He also advocated a "preference" for noncommercial applicants for TV broadcast rights. The fact that few noncommercial operators had applied for licenses in the past was, Washburn believed, attributable to the difficulty such operators faced in competing with commercial operators. He believed a preference for the noncommercial users was essential to producing a more level playing field, because he believed the play of "free and open market" forces would not assist the cause of small, limited-market programming.

Washburn's efforts along these lines didn't get far. The commission on which he served was for the most part not in sympathy with his views. A trend toward deregulation was unexpectedly strengthened with the election of Jimmy Carter. In 1977 the new president appointed Charles Ferris to succeed Chairman Wiley, an appointment that led to less rather than more regulation. The new president's reasons for such deregulation were not the same as those of persons typically considered to be partial to broadcasters, but the result was the same.

The Carter administration's support of deregulation grew partly out of a deep conviction of the new president that the government was bureaucratically top-heavy. It was inefficient and too expensive, and Carter was determined to reduce its size. One of the evils Carter perceived was that the regulated had taken command of the regulators, providing another reason for regulatory agencies to be eliminated or at least reduced in size and scope of operations. Many considered Carter's knowledge of government operations to be woefully minimal and his criticisms of government too simplistic. I find no evidence the Carter people ever gave thought to the effect of their various deregulatory efforts on the lives of those who had been the intended beneficiaries of the regulatory schemes under attack.

Specifically relative to broadcasting, Chairman Ferris supported the deregulation movement, but he was also convinced that amendments to the Communications Act by Congress were essential to any substantial demolition of the regulatory scheme adopted in 1934. That Congress might produce changes in the Communications Act of the kind Ferris thought necessary appeared unlikely and, in fact, were not forthcoming. Although both the Communications and Radio acts had initially been products of legislation, the bulk of what could be identified as broadcast law had been produced by the FCC and the courts. Congress had a fairly cozy relationship with broadcasters; they represented important outlets for congressional campaigns. Broadcasters were generally happy with the way the FCC functioned. Any pressure Congress might feel from them would normally be of the "don't rock the boat" variety. Apparently, one result of this relationship was that "congressional control of broadcast policy by statute [was] . . . of 'relative unimportance.' . . . From 1970 through 1977 Congress enacted only one significant amendment to the Communications Act" (Weinberg 1983, 72).

Illustrative of the serene relationship between broadcasters and the regulatory frame within which they lived was the fate of a seemingly quixotic attempt in 1978 to simplify law applicable to the electronic media. Two members of Congress, Lionel Van Deerlin (as chairman of the House Communications Subcommittee) and his Republican counterpart, Louis Frey, undertook a complete rewrite of the 1934 act. It was a Herculean task.

> If thinkers in the broadcast world . . . conceived of a rewrite, . . . they might have kept the idea to themselves; it surely would have been derided as politically impractical. The perceived power of the broadcast industry, especially the National Association of Broadcasters, was great, and it was the conventional policy within the industry to oppose change. Besides, without any pressure from outsiders to disturb the status quo, Congress had no reason to revamp the 1934 Act. The issues were not compelling and they would have fallen flat back in the home constituencies. (Weinberg 1983, 74-75)

Van Deerlin bucked the trend. He argued to his colleagues that technological change in communications since 1934 had been so substantial that the act was in need of a complete overhaul, commenting that although television had been around for more than 30 years, the word doesn't even appear in the 1934 act![1]

When his effort failed, Van Deerlin was philosophical. Of the lobbyists for the broadcasters who had fought the rewrite, he commented only that "all these folks wanted for their clients was to retain 'a fair advantage.'" He added, "I suppose if there are two people in our home communities we [members of Congress] don't want to offend, it's first the newspaper publishers and second the broadcasters. When we go home to our district, we don't want to be ignored by reporters or by broadcasters. It's our lifeblood. And therefore we tend to listen to these fellows" (Weinberg 1983, 84).

Historian Steve Weinberg has concluded with respect to Van Deerlin's rewrite effort:

> The general public never shared the intense interest [in the rewrite effort] shown by communications lawyers and broadcast industry lobbyists in Washington. That is partly because the general public received little information about the debate. ABC, CBS, and NBC almost totally ignored the story on their newscasts. The *Washington Post,* the *New York Times,* and a few other general circulation newspapers with reporters covering the Federal Communications Commission part-time carried occasional pieces about the debate. But those stories were often buried in the business section, or placed in other back pages of the newspaper. Most members of Congress stayed away from the issue—partly because of its complexity, and partly because of the perception that most voters were happy with the status quo. After all, their televisions entertained them and their telephone service was almost always reliable. (Weinberg 1983, 81)

The rewrite effort failed, and the path of deregulation took a new turn with the election of President Reagan, who appointed Mark Fowler to succeed Ferris. Ferris may have thought congressional action essential to serious deregulation; Fowler did not believe that to be the case.

Consistent with his oft-used slogan "Let the market decide," Mark Fowler was a strong believer in the curative powers of the free market. Though he appeared every inch a conservative, he had nonetheless voted for Lyndon Johnson and viewed himself as a "liberal." He also managed to annoy the networks by ending one set of commission rules they were fond of: the "prime-time access" rules. These had given the networks considerable control over the prime-time programming of their affiliated stations. Fowler leaned toward the Libertarian side of conservatism, placing himself outside the mainstream of Republican conservatism.

The commission's new chairman generally supported complete free speech rights for broadcasters, an end to "unnecessary" rules and paperwork, and reliance on the competitive character of broadcasting for resolution of problems. Consistent with his philosophy, the commission proceeded to eliminate all remaining restrictions blocking identical programming on AM and FM stations under common ownership. He proposed to Congress that it should repeal the fairness doctrine, all public access requirements, and rights of reply as representing policies that infringed broadcasters' First Amendment rights. Under his stewardship the commission undertook a study of the fairness doctrine, which led to a report in 1985 concluding that the doctrine was unconstitutional and that it discourages issue coverage rather than encourages it, the doctrine's ostensible purpose.

Fowler left the commission in 1987, stating in a final interview that if it were only possible, he "would have closed the doors of the FCC for good" when he walked out of the building (Jung 1996, 154). Dennis Patrick, named by Reagan to succeed Fowler, also believed that a truly competitive market existed in broadcasting and should be relied on to solve all broadcasting problems. As the foundation for the direction in which he led the FCC, Patrick dropped not a beat in continuing Fowler's deregulatory pace.

Early in the new chairman's term the license-renewal application form was reduced from a multipage document to a three-by-five postcard. Longstanding requirements that licensee-applicants demonstrate some effort to ascertain the program interests or wishes of their targeted audiences ("ascertainment") were abolished. So was the requirement that broadcasters keep daily programming logs. Citizen groups complained that this would make fighting a license renewal virtually impossible because there would be no record of specific programming to which such opponents objected. Listeners keep no such records. The commission was unmoved.

The single most important decision of the commission under Patrick was to terminate the fairness doctrine requirements that licensees cover controversial issues, and that such coverage be full and impartial. An organization called the Syracuse Peace Council had filed a complaint against a station in upper New York State alleging a violation of the doctrine. The station had carried commercials by private power plants touting the benefits of nuclear-fueled power. The Peace Council, opposed to such plants, complained that the station failed to provide time for reply. The commission agreed this was a violation of the doctrine, but it decided it was time to end the doctrine. Rather than stimulate coverage of controversial issues, as was intended, the doctrine inhibits such coverage, the commission said. The commission further gave its opinion that the doctrine infringes on broadcasters' First Amendment rights notwithstanding the Supreme Court's 1969 opinion to the contrary in the *Red Lion* case. The facts have changed, said the commission.

Responding to this action, a Democratic-controlled Congress enacted legislation placing the fairness doctrine requirements in the Communications Act, but Congress was unable to override President Reagan's veto. Noises have since been made about resurrecting the doctrine, but nothing has happened, and such talk is heard less and less.

The fairness doctrine included three other parts. One of them, the right to answer when one is criticized in the course of coverage of controversial issues, was adopted as a commission rule in 1964. As a formally adopted rule, it can be modified only by commission action, which also follows a prescribed form, including notice of a hearing for consideration of repeal. The commission has not commenced such a procedure, though the rule seems now to be seldom invoked. Another part of the doctrine required broadcaster coverage of ballot initiatives in a thorough and balanced fashion. Some years after 1987 the commission claimed the initiative-coverage part of the doctrine had also ended, a determination that was upheld by a federal court of appeals (*Arkansas AFL-CIO v. FCC* 11 F.3d 1430 [8th Cir., 1993]). The last part of the doctrine is the Zapple component. Like a torn scrap attached to a garment, neither cut off nor sewn back into place, Zapple just hangs there, awaiting its fate. No opportunity for the commission or anyone else to consider its status apparently has yet arisen. It remains "on the books" but its future is clouded. The fairness doctrine as a whole is treated more fully in chapter 11.

Two other problems relative to program content came to the fore in the 1980s. One was the growing incidence of violence and indecent language in broadcasting, particularly television; the second was concern about programs aimed at children. The Supreme Court had many years ago decided that the First Amendment does not protect obscene speech, but nobody has ever come up with a satisfactory definition of "obscene." The late Justice Potter Stewart is famous for his statement claiming that, though unable to define the word, "I know it when I see it" (*Jacobellis v. Ohio* 378 U.S. 184, 187, 1964).

Excluding obscene language from constitutional protection does not exclude all language that might be considered offensive. "Indecent" language covers a category of words that necessarily includes the obscene, but not all indecent language is obscene. In print media, indecent language that is *not* obscene *is* protected by the First Amendment. Does that protection extend to the same language when used in broadcasting?

This question was answered by the Supreme Court in 1978 in *Pacifica Foundation v. FCC* 438 U.S. 726. Pacifica had carried a comedy routine of George Carlin's intended to demonstrate absurd aspects in our common use of vulgar words. The routine used words like, "shit," "cunt," and "fuck." The commission received only a single complaint about the program and sent Pacifica an admonitory letter, with a copy in the commission's file. Deciding to make this a test case, Pacifica appealed the commission action, alleging that it infringed Pacifica's First Amendment rights.

The Supreme Court agreed that in print the routine's words would be protected by the First Amendment. But broadcasting, said the court, is a different matter. Broadcasting is not entitled to the same First Amendment rights as print, so the government may restrict use of indecent language over the air. Such restriction is necessary because broadcasting is "uniquely pervasive," and because the program in the case was at a time children were likely to be listening. After that decision, language often considered indecent was heard less frequently on radio and television—for a while. There are indications that trend may have been reversed.

On the other hand, explicitly suggestive sexual material and violence, never in short supply, didn't even take a dip and are now thought to be on the increase. There have been numerous studies of the effects on children of violence portrayed on TV. Although such studies appear to lack evidence even approaching the overwhelming, most lend support to the view that violent programming can cause undesirable conduct by minors. However, defining "violence" or "sexually explicit material" in a way to make any prohibition work, even if constitutionally permissible, seems a daunting task.

No one would state a wish that broadcasting carry visuals and language suitable only for children. For their part, some broadcasters engage in self-censorship, whereas others lean on their First Amendment rights in hope of avoiding *any* interference. Faced with competition from cable, broadcasters of all minds often feel caught between the devil and a hard place. Of course, "sympathy" for the broadcasters' dilemma in face of cable is also useful to broadcasters in dealing with new efforts to control these aspects of program content.[2]

One lobbying group, Action for Children's Television, approached some of these problems in a different way. The group focused on education in its efforts to improve the quality of programs designed for children, and its effort was largely responsible for the Children's Television Act of 1990. This law limits the advertising permissible in children's programming, but more important, it mandates that television licensees shall carry programs that serve the educational and informational ("cognitive/intellectual or emotional/social") needs of children. No specific quantities of program content were prescribed by the statute. It is for the commission to determine whether there has been compliance when a television broadcast license is considered for renewal. Clearly, the assumption was that that programming intended to satisfy the statute would minimize both violence and explicit sex.

Eight years after the Children's Television Act became law, the consensus seemed to be that little had changed. There may be a few more programs whose claim to serve the needs of children as required by the act is not utterly absurd, but no license has failed to be renewed for reasons of noncompliance, nor has any renewal applicant even been admonished in the course of being granted its renewal. The amount of time devoted to advertising in children's programs also seems to have been unaffected by the very general remedial requirements of that law.

Another problem of the 1980s concerned the relationship between cable and broadcasting. Ambiguous from the beginning, the alliance between the two was marked by a kind of love/hate relationship. As CATV grew, corporations that were involved in broadcasting and that emphasized the corporate "bottom line" hedged their positions by investing in cable, giving rise to important differences between broadcasters having cable interests and those that did not. This divergence hampered formation of a united broadcaster front to deal with conflicts between cable and use of the spectrum.

Congressional efforts to resolve some of the problems began with adoption of the 1976 Copyright Act. Reform of copyright law had begun ten years earlier, but progress was stymied by disputes between recording companies and music publishers, and between copyright owners in general and cable. The issue involving cable rose from the fact that cable programming consisted almost entirely of programs picked up from network broadcasts. The programs were copyrighted, but cable paid nothing to the programs' owners for their use. The networks were of two minds about the issue. In its early days cable operations enhanced the audience for network programs by exposing programs to folks who would not otherwise be reached. This was good for sponsors and for the rates they could be charged. As cable grew and began to gain a larger share of the viewing audience, even producing programming of its own, the attitude of many broadcasters changed.

The position of broadcasters was further complicated by the fact that many programs' copyrights were not owned by the network, but by the producer of a show. This entity (person, partnership, or corporation) probably had contractual obligations to writers (as might the networks with respect to shows they owned) that they might feel insufficiently honored by cable's "free" ride. Music and public performance rights were also involved. An earlier attempt had been made to use part of the existing copyright law, the 1906 act, to force cable to pay for use of copyrighted programming, but that attempt failed when the Supreme Court ruled against the copyright owners in *Fortnightly v. United Artists TV* 392 U.S. 390 (1968). As a result copyright owners pressured Congress for redress in the new copyright bill pending in Washington since 1966.

The copyright question was eventually resolved by provisions in the 1976 act allowing cable to utilize any copyrighted material originating in broadcasting without having to obtain specific permission in each case. This is called a "compulsory license," compulsory because the copyright owner has no say as to whether the license will be granted or not. In turn, cable companies were required to make annual payments to a copyright fund to be divided among the various copyright interests according to prescribed formulas. The administrative details get complicated, as do the methods adopted for making all of this work, and the methods have undergone modification since 1976. Such matters are beyond the scope of this book. The important points are that although cable must now pay for use of copyrighted material, no copyright owner has a right to prevent such use once the work has been publicly performed, and copyright owners now have a "partner," the government, in setting and collecting the fees cable must pay for use of their works.

As the years have gone by, there has been unhappiness on both sides with respect to this solution to the copyright problem, but no one has come up with a better idea, though the rates to be paid, as provided in the 1976 act, have been occasionally tinkered with

The dispute between broadcasters and cable concerning intellectual property rights was not the only matter to concern Congress. In the early 1980s, as cable was becoming a greater political power than in its early mom-and-pop days, it grew increasingly restive by virtue of being subjected to regulation by the hundreds of communities that franchised it. Cable operations sought to be relieved at least of local regulation of subscriber rates. Negotiating such rates with numerous municipalities at different times, each negotiation unrelated to another, seemed to present considerable hardship. Many cable operations concluded that dealing with a single regulator at the federal level would be better than dealing with thousands of small regulatory agencies. Congress responded by enacting the Cable Communications Policy Act of 1984.

Here another drama unfolded. Congress was controlled by Democrats; most FCC commissioners had been appointed by President Reagan and seemed hell-bent on dismantling the regulatory agency they were legally charged to administer. If cable was to find some relief from being subject to rate regulation by myriad small communities, the industry could not simply be "turned loose," yet the obvious candidate for uniform regulation at the federal level, the FCC, was "not to be trusted." The result was a Byzantine system freeing cable from most rate control for two years, to be followed by a complex combination of controls by local franchising agencies whose authority would depend on whether the cable company was or was not faced with "significant competition." The definition of "significant competition" was to be formulated by the FCC.

Some aspects of the 1984 Policy Act have survived; the rate deregulation/regulation scheme is not one of them. Deregulation brought complaints from constituents that rates were soaring, complaints that provided much of the incentive for adoption of the Cable Television Consumer Protection and Competition Act of 1992. This act imposed substantial new regulatory features on cable. Interestingly, with one notable exception, the cable industry has not complained that its constitutional rights, specifically of the First Amendment type, have been infringed.

Cable might have raised First Amendment issues with respect to *local* regulation. Such a suit or suits would probably have been extraordinarily difficult to maintain, if only for logistical reasons. Replacement of local regulation with a single federal regulatory system would therefore likely have appeared attractive enough to discourage attacking the new system out of fear that success would only lead to restoration of the former, less desirable system. It may well have been a dilemma like the dilemma faced by broadcasters who did not wish to undermine the licensing scheme out of fear of a return to chaos. Those broadcasters saw no alternative solution to that provided by the Communications Act.

One requirement of the 1992 act that cable operators did attack was the so-called "must carry" provision. Ultimately they lost. "Must carry" is discussed in greater detail in chapter 10.

Reed Hundt became the first commission chairman named by President Clinton. He made statements indicating his intent to return to the more activist and interventionist role played by former commissioners like Newton Minow. Such rhetoric was blunted by the 1992 midterm elections, which gave control of both houses of Congress to the Republicans. Hundt probably also found himself much occupied with problems of implementing the 1992 Cable Act, and his workload increased dramatically when Congress adopted the 1996 Telecommunications Act. Chapter 14 is devoted to considering that statute. Hundt left the commission in 1997 to be replaced by Bill Kennard, whose job is to lead the commission in wrestling with implementation of the 1996 Telecommunications Act.

Notes

1. Van Deerlin thought the commission guilty of unreasonable flip-flops. In an article he authored that appeared in the *San Diego Tribune* of April 16, 1987, titled "'Fairness Doctrine' Negates Constitutional Protection," he described the *Mayflower* decision (correctly) as having banned broadcaster editorials, while describing the later fairness doctrine (incorrectly) as having *required* such editorials. In fact, the doctrine required only that opinions expressed in editorials, *if any,* be balanced by expression of opposing views.

2. In *Reno v. ACLU* 138 L.Ed.2d 874 (1997), the Supreme Court held unconstitutional provisions of the 1996 Telecommunications Act intended to criminalize use of "indecent" language, or proposal of indecent acts, or presentation of indecent visuals on the Internet.

CHAPTER 9

Television versus FM

Television became a practical possibility in the 1930s, but the advent of World War II delayed its arrival for general public use. When such use became a reality following the war, the industry and the FCC faced new problems. One was TV's relationship to FM radio, a static-free system developed about the same time. The two were ultimately in conflict with each other, and the champions of TV won.

As with many aspects of broadcasting, the pace of television's development may be credited to David Sarnoff. The intensity of purpose with which RCA's president pursued his goal of making television a commercial reality was a major factor in determining the fate of FM, in ending Armstrong's friendship with Sarnoff, and probably, at least to some extent, in leading to Armstrong's decision to take his life in 1954. High prices to pay, but prices that were unknown to Sarnoff when he took steps intended to advance the cause of television.

Amplitude modulation, the first form of broadcasting, was always afflicted by static. Thinking like an engineer, Howard Armstrong considered static to be broadcasting's most serious problem, and in 1914 he began laboratory research to find a solution. In 1922 he predicted that the problem of static would one day be solved. It was, and he did it.

In 1935 Armstrong paid a visit to RCA, where he invited David Sarnoff to his lab to witness a major event. Certain that something big was afoot, Sarnoff ordered his car from the garage, and the two friends went together. At the laboratory Sarnoff saw an array of equipment that produced clear sound with a complete absence of static. "This is not just an invention," said the impressed Sarnoff. "This is a revolution!"

Sarnoff's enthusiasm for Armstrong's frequency modulation invention did not last long. He had promised Armstrong research support as well as a transmission tower atop the RCA building. The latter was supplied; the former was not. Eventually even use of the tower ended, and Armstrong was told to remove his equipment. The most serious blow, however, was RCA's successful campaign to persuade the FCC to relegate FM radio broadcasting to a "lesser" part of the spectrum than AM, a part that generated waves few existing radios could detect.

Why had RCA done this? Sarnoff, who had been president of RCA since 1930, had a number of concerns. Convinced that the future of broadcasting lay in television, he intended that every available research dollar should be used to develop that medium; diversion of resources to further radio broadcasting by FM was, he thought, wasteful investment in a sideshow. Second, Sarnoff was concerned that expansion of FM broadcasting would require the listening public to junk old radio equipment and buy new sets designed to receive FM signals. If television arrived a short time later, consumers would again need to buy new equipment. Neither development was likely to endear the consumer to RCA. These were important considerations for the president of the major radio producer in the nation.

Sarnoff doubtless also took into account government regulation of broadcasting, and FTC concerns with unfair trade practices. He had also to be mindful of possible new technological developments that were being announced almost weekly, not to mention coverage of the corporation's conduct by a fickle press. With so much to balance, it was not surprising for Sarnoff to focus on television, the ultimate prize. Such considerations probably did not occur to Armstrong. Ever the scientist, he would have been totally focused on the marvel of static-free reception. Undoubtedly, pride of invention was also a factor in his single-minded pursuit of the development of FM radio.

Sarnoff's conduct toward Armstrong at that time seemed to many unnecessarily harsh. As development of TV went forward at RCA, FM appeared to offer its best sound system. Unwilling or unable to make peace with Armstrong on terms Sarnoff considered satisfactory, RCA's engineers tinkered with Armstrong's technology and purported to develop a "different" FM, original enough to qualify for a separate patent. Armstrong once again found himself in patent litigation, this time with RCA, led by his erstwhile friend, David Sarnoff.

With respect to Armstrong, Sarnoff may have been "playing dirty." With respect to his shareholders, perhaps he could not appropriately have done otherwise. In any case, opposing RCA's wealth against Armstrong's limited resources, RCA managed to drag out Armstrong's patent suit for years. The corporation was also successful in causing the FCC to adopt measures seriously crimping the use of FM. In 1944, in anticipation of the end of World War II and preparing to add TV and FM to the spectrum already being used by AM, the FCC held hearings to determine the appropriate bands for each.

The networks had made noises to the effect that sunspots could disrupt FM signals. To protect those signals, corporate engineers suggested that FM be moved from its then current spectrum position of 45 to 50 megacycles to one higher on the band. Because existing transmitting equipment and radios were geared for FM broadcasting at the position it then occupied, such a shift could prove disastrous for FM. According to an account of the events described in Tom Lewis's 1991 *Empire of the Air: The Men Who Made Radio,* the threatened move wasn't seen by the FM forces to be serious until a War Department engineer, who had also formerly been on the FCC staff, testified that sunspots could indeed interfere with FM signals. The commission was convinced, and at the urging of CBS and RCA, proceeded to relocate FM between 88 and 108 megacycles. FM's former location, 45 to 50 megacycles, was allocated to TV, as requested by the two radio giants. The sound signal for TV was also transmitted by FM, but no one—Armstrong included—apparently thought to worry about sunspot interference with this use.

Two other actions taken by the commission were highly detrimental to FM radio. One was intended to reduce the reach of signals to prevent an FM station from serving more than a single community by limiting the power permitted for FM transmissions. Pushed by the networks, particularly CBS, as "democratizing" FM, this idea had the effect of pauperizing FM stations that had no tie to an AM station. FM stations affiliated with networks didn't care. They had sister AM stations whose wider-ranging transmissions carried the advertising of network programs, revenues that supported both the AM and FM stations. Only FM stations operating alone would be crippled when advertisers refused to buy advertising limited to small populations already blanketed with the commercial messages of AM stations affiliated with networks.

The other network coup was a requirement that FM stations that also operated an AM station carry the same programming on both frequencies. CBS purported to agree with Armstrong's prediction that FM would replace AM, but during the transition from AM to FM, CBS said, it would be important not to make AM radios already in the hands of consumers obsolete. Similarly, the FCC should assure new FM radio users that they would not lose their favorite AM programs; ergo, programming should be the same on both. The result eliminated any reason advertisers might have for advertising on FM, as it would only duplicate advertising already placed on AM programs. The commission saw no ulterior motives when it approved this policy, dealing FM broadcasting a serious blow.

In spite of these setbacks, Armstrong continued his crusade for FM. With a small coterie of dedicated enthusiasts, he attempted to keep FM radio alive and viable. He also undertook expensive demonstrations in an effort to spike rumors that FM signals were affected by sunspots and could not be transmitted long distances. He became increasingly single-minded in his purpose and increasingly depressed by failures and by what he saw as betrayal by his "friends" at RCA.

Impoverished and depressed, Armstrong committed suicide in 1954. It is perhaps a measure of Sarnoff's feelings of guilt that, when informed by one of his close associates of Armstrong's death, an obviously shocked Sarnoff said simply "I did not kill Howard Armstrong"!

Armstrong's widow pursued the patent infringement suit her husband had commenced against RCA and other users of FM technology. Ultimately she won substantial recompense from all parties, though there is evidence that the amount recovered from RCA was close to the sum Sarnoff had offered Armstrong in settlement of his claim against RCA, years before his death.

Close on the heels of World War II's end, television began a phenomenal growth. The three major networks quickly acquired licenses for telecasting in the nation's most important markets. There ensued such a flood of license applications that the FCC felt inundated and in need of slowing the rush. In 1948 it announced a freeze on TV license applications; no more were to be considered until the freeze was lifted. The freeze may well have allowed the FCC to get its house in order, but it also was manna from heaven for the already-licensed networks. Covering the major markets as they did, the networks were able to establish themselves in the public mind as *the* purveyors of TV programming. (This position was threatened only recently by the growth of cable, requiring the FCC's "clients" to add to their arsenal a new weapon called "must carry." See chapter 10.)

When the freeze was lifted in 1951, the networks' position was strongly entrenched. New TV licensees almost invariably became affiliated with one of the three networks, assuring such licensees success in viable markets. The only applicant for one or two stations in Austin, Texas, was the wife of the future president, Lyndon Baines Johnson. How she knew of the TV availability and was the sole applicant are questions without clear answers. Winning the TV award was a follow-up to her acquisition of an

Austin radio station in 1943 under conditions indicating that LBJ employed the political muscle of his popular and powerful fellow Texan, the Speaker of the House, Sam Rayburn. Johnson always claimed the stations were acquired by his wife, were owned and run by her, and that he neither knew anything about them nor profited from them. But it was Johnson himself who in the mid 1940s, following purchase of the radio station, went to see CBS's William Paley and obtained a coveted CBS affiliation for his wife's station. The entire episode bespeaks a close relationship between the FCC commissioners and their masters in Congress. The Johnson family is now wealthy. One source of that wealth is the Austin TV stations.[1]

By 1955 TV had supplanted radio as the broadcasting medium. Americans might look to radio for music to accompany their leisure-time activities, but they looked to TV for their primary at-home entertainment. Furthermore, according to polls, the great majority of Americans acquired most if not all news about their communities, the nation, and the world from TV. The reach of broadcasting was of unimaginable power. That power was only to increase.

Notes

1. Accounts of the acquisition of the Austin stations by the Johnsons are provided in Dallek 1991 and Caro 1990, chap. 6.

CHAPTER 10

Cable and Other Media

I ssues involved in the regulation of broadcasting grew in complexity with the advent of cable. Although cable has the capacity to deliver to our homes the same programming delivered by broadcasters, no license from the FCC is required to do so. This chapter examines how cable produced problems for broadcasters and the resulting integration of cable into the regulatory pattern for the electromagnetic spectrum.

Cable first emerged as small one-or-two-person operations, using cable or wire to extend the reach of broadcast signals into terrain where reception by typical radios or television sets was unsatisfactory. The FCC first considered whether it had any jurisdiction, or obligation, to regulate cable in 1952. It concluded it did not, as "cable" was not "broadcasting." Broadcast licensees apparently did not view cable as a threat but as an extension of the reach of programs that would increase potential audiences and justify higher advertising revenues. This symbiotic relationship did not last.

Cable operations graduated from their mom-and-pop status and knocked at the door of the big boys. Southwest Cable Company, operating in San Diego, began to import programs via antenna from Los Angeles rather than carrying the programs of the local stations, which had been the normal operating procedure for cable. San Diego broadcasters complained to the FCC because this threatened to diminish the size of their audiences, endangering advertising rates. Although not the first complaint the commission received from its licensee/clients with respect to the development of cable, it was the first that brought to the Supreme Court a question of federal authority to regulate cable.

In response to complaints from San Diego broadcasters, the commission made a rule forbidding cable systems from importing distant signals.

101

Southwestern contended the FCC had no jurisdiction over cable and appealed the decision. On the appeal, the cable company relied solely on the language and purpose of the Communications Act to sustain its position, failing to argue an infringement of its First Amendment rights. Under the statute, cable needed no license from the FCC. Therefore, said Southwestern, the commission was without power to tell cable what to do. In the decision, *Southwestern Cable Co. v. FCC* 392 U.S. 157 (1968), the Supreme Court pointed out that although the act required that only broadcasters be licensed, it also expressed the intent of Congress to regulate all communication by wireless or by wire. Southwestern conceded it used wire.

Though unable to give specific definition to the extent of FCC jurisdiction over cable, the Court defined such jurisdiction as including acts reasonably necessary to effectuate the FCC's statutory duty to regulate TV. Whatever the extent of such power over cable, said the Court, it certainly included the authority to make the nonimportation order to which Southwestern objected. Maybe Southwestern would have lost anyway, but by not making a First Amendment argument, it surely made the government's job easier, giving the FCC an edge and a victory that validated its entry into the field of cable regulation. It is always harder to eliminate a complex regulatory scheme in place than to prevent its introduction in the first place.

The Supreme Court was called upon two or three more times to clarify the extent found in *Southwestern* of the commission's jurisdiction over cable. Only once did a case raise a First Amendment argument. The cable company won that case for a reason unrelated to the Constitution, so the Court never had to address the constitutional issue. It is worth pointing out here that the Supreme Court always avoids deciding a constitutional question in a case unless it must do so. If the Court determines that the party raising a constitutional question will prevail on a different, nonconstitutional ground, the Court's judgment will be so grounded and it will not consider the constitutional question.

In 1984 Congress enacted the Cable Communications Policy Act, which bestowed on the commission specific authority to regulate cable. This grant, rather than the jurisdictional basis found by the Supreme Court in the *Southwestern* case, thereafter became the mat on which cable operators and the government wrestled their regulatory disputes. No cable operator—and by then there were some big ones like Turner Broadcasting System—tried to test the constitutionality of the 1984 Cable Act and its grant of power to the commission to regulate cable. This was probably because cable operators generally, and the more affluent ones in particular (who might be able to finance such expensive litigation), believed that they got more from the act than they lost. What they got was a measure of freedom from control by local governments.

Because cable must be physically located somewhere, and that "somewhere" is virtually always in a public right-of-way, permission from local authorities was essential for laying or stringing the cable. Such permission was given in the form of a franchise of limited duration under which a local authority reserved the power to regulate the operator's rates to its subscribers and charged a fee for use of the right-of-way, customarily a percentage of the operator's take. Regulation of cable, then, had existed before the *Southwestern* decision or passage of the 1984 act, but no *federal* regulation had existed. As the business of cable grew and became more lucrative, one entity might own a number of cable operations, each having its subscriber rates regulated by a different local authority and in a different manner. One thing that could be counted on in the 1960s was that tax revenues for local governments would diminish. Passage of California's Proposition 13 symbolized widespread resistance to taxes, and governments dug deep for other sources of income. Cable provided one.

On balance, many operators considered federal regulation, which eliminated the locals, to be a "cable relief" bill. The 1984 act limited local power to regulate subscriber rates for two years. Thereafter no such regulation was permitted unless, using a standard to be developed by the FCC, the franchising authority found the cable operator to be without effective competition. The act also made it difficult for local franchising governments to deny franchise renewal to cable operators, a possibly more serious blow to local authorities in that it bestowed on holders of cable franchises a right to retain them so long as the local government was unable to show a substantial breach of the franchise agreement. The 1984 act traded a known, but varied and often onerous, regulation by locals for an unknown, but probably more "manageable," regulation by the FCC. It might have been seen as more manageable because in dealing with the FCC, "organized" cable could often stand as one entity, represented by those who lobbied for the richest among them, working in Congress in the interest of all. Not to be overlooked, the 1984 act also placed a cap on the amount the local authorities could charge for operating privilege franchises.

Even before adoption of the 1984 act, but relying on the *Southwestern* case, the commission adopted a number of policy requirements applicable to cable, one of which was the so-called "must carry" rule. This rule mandated that cable operations beyond a certain size devote some of their channels to the programs of local TV stations. Maybe because cable already complied with "must carry," or maybe because no cable operator was rich enough or interested enough in making constitutional law to finance a lawsuit, no one challenged this rule for more than ten years. Then, in 1977, Quincy Cable, a Washington State operator, was fined by the commission for violating it. Quincy appealed, alleging the rule infringed its First Amendment rights. The court of appeals agreed, and its decision in *Quincy v. FCC* 768 F.2d 1434 (1985) invalidated the rule.

Broadcasters were galvanized into action; pressure was brought on Congress, which in turn "advised" the commission to reenact a "must carry" rule that would be upheld. This "advice," however, came from a Democrat-controlled Congress and was addressed to an FCC that was controlled by Reagan appointees dedicated to deregulation. On the other hand, Republican members of Congress also had friends in the broadcasting world, friends who called on these Republicans to support the congressional "advice" that had been directed to the FCC. The commission made an attempt to adopt a revised rule, which subsequently was tested and held unconstitutional by the court of appeals in *Century Communications v. FCC* 835 F.2d 292 (1987). The Supreme Court did not review either decision.

Not long after passage of the 1984 act, consumers began to complain that their cable rates were skyrocketing. And consumers had more votes than did cable operators. The 1984 act's weakening of regulation of subscriber rates seemed to have been a mistake, which Congress rectified in adopting the 1992 Cable Television Consumer Protection and Competition Act (the "1992 Cable Act"). Local power to regulate subscriber rates was at least partially restored, and "must carry" was made a statutory requirement. No longer representing merely a policy decision of the FCC, the obligation of cable to carry local TV programs was now part of a statute enacted by the Congress of the United States.

A federal court of appeals had on two occasions held the "must carry" requirement unconstitutional as infringing the First Amendment rights of cable companies. Armed with these decisions, a group of cable operators, led by Turner Broadcasting System, brought an action to test once again the constitutionality of "must carry," now part of the 1992 Cable Act. This suit was heard by a three-judge panel of a federal district court, as Congress had required.

In *Turner Broadcasting System, Inc. V. FCC,* the district court held that "must carry" did not violate the First Amendment rights of cable operators, a decision that the Supreme Court (in "*Turner* I," 512 U.S. 622, 1994) reversed for technical reasons. On reconsideration the district court again upheld "must carry," a decision this time affirmed (*Turner* II) by the

Supreme Court (137 L. Ed.2d 369, 1997). After two victories for cable (even before *Turner* I), in the end cable lost where it counted most. How could this have happened? The answer to this question requires examination of some Supreme Court decisions in other First Amendment cases.

A 1913 Florida statute was the subject of *Tornillo v. Miami Herald*, a case discussed in chapter 7. The statute required newspapers to give political candidates space to reply to a newspaper's criticism. Generally unenforced because Florida law enforcement officials considered it to contravene the First Amendment, it was invoked in 1970 by a candidate for the state assembly, one Pat Tornillo, who had been criticized by the *Miami Herald*. Tornillo demanded space to reply, the paper refused, and Tornillo brought suit. Though the statute clearly affected newspaper content, the Florida Supreme Court decided it was valid, reasoning (in concepts perhaps borrowed from the U.S. Supreme Court decision in *Red Lion*) that the statute *furthered* First Amendment interests by providing the public with more, not less, information of importance.

The U.S. Supreme Court (*Miami Herald v. Tornillo* 418 U.S. 241, 1974) reversed the Florida court's decision. Describing the statute as direct interference with a newspaper's editorial judgment, the nation's highest court said it clearly violated the guarantees of the First Amendment. The reasoning of the Florida Supreme Court drew not even a hint of support, nor was there any reference to the high court's earlier *Red Lion* opinion. But using some of the reasoning of the losing side in *Red Lion,* the Court opined that such a requirement as Florida's could inhibit that robust, uninhibited journalism the First Amendment was designed to protect.

In *Red Lion* the Court had upheld the fairness doctrine. Because no party to that case asserted a right to broadcast without holding a federal license, and because there were only so many licenses available from the FCC, the Court was unwilling to find that the fairness doctrine's interference with the broadcasters' editorial decisions infringed First Amendment rights. How could it if one must be licensed to broadcast in the first place?

So in *Red Lion,* because not everyone who might wish to be licensed to broadcast can be, the Court was able to emphasize the "trustee" capacity of those who win licenses. Being licensed, said the Court, justifies imposition of an obligation to voice the ideas of the unlicensed—for the benefit of *listeners* as well as for the benefit of the unlicensed. The First Amendment rights of listeners, said the Court in *Red Lion*, are more important than those of broadcasters. At the same time, the authority of the government is not unlimited. Broadcasters are not without First Amendment rights, said the justices, but what those rights may be is not very clear.

Except as that amendment has been held to prevent Congress from banning editorializing by tax-supported "public" radio, First Amendment rights of broadcasters remain murky.

One proposition for which *Red Lion* clearly stands is that broadcasters' First Amendment rights are lesser than those of other media outlets. The scope of such rights for print media was decided in the *Tornillo* case as being quite extensive. Consideration of the nature of First Amendment rights of cable came next, but the first case presenting such an issue was an oddball one arising in Los Angeles. That city had limited to one the number of cable services to be permitted in south central Los Angeles, state law having given municipal bodies the power to make such decisions. Besides, it was generally assumed municipalities had pretty much an absolute right (so long as not exercised arbitrarily) to do so. After all, local governments had always controlled who could dig up their streets, hang wires in their rights-of-way, and otherwise control private use of public property. Such matters fell within what was called the "police power."

The city had invited bids to provide south central Los Angeles with cable service; bids were received and an award was made. A cable operator who had not participated in the bidding process applied for a license to service the same area. This application was turned down and the applicant sued the city, alleging infringement of its First Amendment rights. The city won in the lower courts, but in *Preferred Communications, Inc. v. City of Los Angeles* (476 U.S. 488, 1985) the Supreme Court sent the case back for further proceedings. The city had claimed that letting just anyone dig up its streets would create an intolerable burden for the municipality and its citizens, and that hanging unlimited numbers of wires from poles would be an aesthetic disaster. The cable company's response was that these matters could be worked out. There had been no trial dealing with such issues because the city had won in the lower courts on the theory that its rights were absolute. That was wrong, said the Supreme Court; the cable operator has First Amendment rights that are also important and must be taken into account in evaluating the importance of the city's claims. A trial was required to determine whether the city's concerns were sufficient to defeat cable's First Amendment rights. The case was ultimately resolved in lower courts, so the issues were not again brought to the nation's highest court.

Although this case didn't settle much, it raised important questions, some of which are relevant to this discussion. We have already seen that two Court decisions struck down the "must carry" rule as infringing free speech rights of cable, whereas on the "third strike" cable was "out." We have also seen that in the *Preferred* case the Supreme Court held that cable operators have First Amendment rights that might conceivably *require* local governments to allow such operators to place transmission lines in public property. In light of this history, why was it that cable lost its fight against "must carry" on its third, and crucial, try?

In that third try, the *Turner* case, the government urged that cable should be considered in the same league with broadcasters so far as First Amendment rights are concerned, and governed by the *Red Lion* decision, severely restricting cable operators' rights. The Court rejected that approach, asserting that spectrum scarcity is basic to defining the rule for broadcasters and is not a factor relative to cable. Having thus successfully resisted use of a *Red Lion* approach to resolving the issues, the cable interests argued that the case to which the Court should look is *Tornillo*. The First Amendment rights of cable, they asserted, should be identical to those of print media.

During argument of the *Turner* case, the government had pointed out that cable usually lacks competition in the areas it serves. Notwithstanding the possibilities suggested by the Supreme Court's decision in the *Preferred Communications* case, the facts are that in the vast majority of situations only one cable company is available to serve customers in each market. When cable operators sought applicability of the rule of *Tornillo*, the government emphasized this monopoly status to distinguish cable companies from dailies like the *Miami Herald*. Even if cable does enjoy aspects of monopoly status, retorted the cable parties, that's beside the point because most newspapers also enjoy a monopoly status in their geographical areas.

Considering these contentions, the Court acknowledged that newspapers may indeed be monopolistic in the areas they serve, but, relative to cable, with a difference. A newspaper enjoying a monopoly cannot keep out of its area newspapers from other parts of the country. Cable operators, on the other hand, by virtue of their hookup to the subscriber's TV set, have complete control of what is shown on the screen. They are thus "gatekeepers" in a way newspapers are not; they *can* keep off the subscriber's TV set all programming other than that transmitted by the cable company. In conclusion, the Court decided that neither *Red Lion* nor *Tornillo* applied to this case. Asserting that each medium of communication presents its own problems with respect to application of the First Amendment, for determining cable's rights the court turned to a formula that had been developed in *O'Brien v. U.S.* (391 U.S. 367, 1968).

The rule of the *O'Brien* case arose out of prosecution of a student opponent of the Vietnam War for destroying his draft card. He had burned his card in public to protest the war. Destruction or alteration of the draft card was an offense under the Selective Service Act. O'Brien argued that his act was "speech" and thus was protected by the First Amendment. Treating O'Brien's conduct as though it were speech, the Court set forth a rule for determining the validity of government regulation that indirectly has the effect of restricting speech. Such regulation has to be in pursuance of a legitimate and substantial government interest; it cannot be specifically directed at speech; and it must further the government interest while producing as little restriction on speech as possible.

Applying that rule in the *Turner* case, the Court accepted the government's claim (apparently without being seriously disputed by the cable parties) that saving "free" TV is a substantial and legitimate government interest, with "free TV" understood to mean TV with no subscription fee. The Court then discussed the two remaining issues: whether cable threatened free TV and whether "must carry" would likely lessen that threat while being the least intrusive restriction on cable operations. Answering both in the affirmative and concluding that "must carry" was "content neutral," that is, not directed at any particular speech (a conclusion with which the dissenters disagreed), the Court upheld the constitutionality of the "must carry" rule.

The reasoning of the Court is thought provoking. A TV set can have a number of cable connections if a number of cable services are available. Although the *O'Brien* formula might still provide the tool for deciding, if more than one cable operator is available to subscribers (in light of the decision in *Preferred*), does that change the *Turner* result derived from application of the *O'Brien* rule? Satellite dishes have decoders. A satellite dish owner is not restricted as to the number of decoding services to which to subscribe, so what are the First Amendment rights of satellite service providers? If there is only one cable company, but one or more satellite services are available, does that affect the *Turner* result? How many subscribers to a cable company (without other cable competitors) who also have satellite dishes must there be before such a question becomes relevant? There are many variations on these themes, many questions—but few answers.

The information highway being developed combines a variety of links (cable, wire, satellite dishes, and so on) used for phone calls, cable, wireless transmission. These are used by all sorts of providers, singly or in some combination. Computer services are also involved. Who has what First Amendment rights will be a complex matter to work out. Courts are not well designed to develop long-term policy, which requires extensive hearings, research, and the input of many parties. Yet it is a weakness of our legislative system that the courts are likely to be left to make complex determinations precisely because Congress prefers to avoid making decisions that might offend one or more constituent groups.

Finally, we know that all means of mass communication are limited by financial considerations, despite the fact that, rightly or wrongly, money questions have largely been classified as legally irrelevant. Money aside, we've seen the factors so far used by the Supreme Court in deciding whether and when some government regulation of speech is permissible under the First Amendment. The limits of these rules have not been delineated. They may never be.

CHAPTER 11

The Fall of the Fairness Doctrine

Imposition on broadcasters of the duty to be guided by the fairness doctrine represented the most important government effort to make broadcasting serve the public interest. Originating in the FCC's decision in the *Mayflower* case, which banned editorializing by FCC licensees, a ban lifted some years later, the doctrine evolved into a *requirement* that licensees provide coverage of issues of public concern. Such coverage was to air all sides, and to afford persons criticized in the course of such coverage an opportunity to reply at no cost. The third provision, the right of reply, was incorporated in a rule formally adopted by the commission in 1967. The first two parts of the doctrine continued simply as commission policy.

The doctrine embodied some ambiguities. An often-heard defense for protection of free speech is that it is required to place *all* ideas in the "marketplace of ideas," so that truth will prevail. John Milton, credited with the early statement of this idea, once said of "Truth," "Let her and Falsehood grapple; whoever knew Truth put to the worse in a free and open encounter?" This oft-quoted sentence expressing a pretty sentiment contains the seeds of its own falsehood. One can know that "Truth" prevailed over "Falsehood" only if one had known "the truth" in advance. I would also venture that falsehood has often prevailed over truth, but perhaps that means no more than that the encounter was not both "free" and "open."

In any event, the fairness doctrine was intended to elicit from broadcasting an educational service whereby citizens might be kept informed about matters of public concern; they would be made aware of all sides of an issue so that they could make up their own minds about the best course to be taken. To this end the emphasis seems to have been on the quantity, rather than quality, of information. The commission did not judge when

111

the information supplied made further information unnecessary, though questions about the "fullness" of coverage and the adequacy of reply rights remained open. Such questions will be further examined in chapter 13.

The doctrine clearly interferes with broadcasters' speech, but no legal assault on it came until the 1964 presidential campaign between Barry Goldwater and Lyndon Johnson. During that campaign a book critical of Goldwater was written by one Fred Cook. Titled *Goldwater, Extremist on the Right,* it was reviewed on a Philadelphia radio station by the Reverend Billy Hargis, a well-known spokesman for right-wing political views. The radio station was owned by Red Lion Broadcasting Company, whose management was also dedicated to "conservative" causes. Hargis's review was highly critical of the book and its author, whom Hargis labeled a communist and other derogatory things. When Cook heard of the broadcast, he demanded an opportunity to reply and the station refused. Cook complained to the commission, which ordered Red Lion to make time available for Cook's reply. Red Lion appealed the FCC order to the federal courts, alleging that it violated the station's First Amendment rights.

Following commission action incorporating the right of reply into a formally adopted FCC rule, and after the Cook/Hargis episode, the Radio Television News Directors Association (RTNDA) brought suit in federal court for an injunction to prevent enforcement of the new rule on the grounds that it violated First Amendment rights of association members. Appeals from both the suit commenced by Red Lion and that brought by the RTNDA reached the Supreme Court at the same time. The two were consolidated for decision in *Red Lion Broadcasting Co., Inc. v. FCC* 395 U.S. 367, and a decision came down in 1969.

In the discussion of this case in chapter 7, I pointed out that no party questioned the power of the government to require a license to engage in broadcasting, and the Court's decision in upholding the constitutionality of the fairness doctrine clearly assumed the validity of the licensing scheme as set forth in the Communications Act. Of course, even within the context of licensing there is a legitimate question as to whether the doctrine infringes broadcasters' First Amendment rights, and it was that question that the Court addressed.

Citing the *NBC* case, the Court reiterated that there is no First Amendment right to a license to broadcast. This also means, the Court continued, that a "license permits broadcasting, but the licensee has no constitutional right to be the one who holds the license or to monopolize a frequency to the exclusion of his fellow citizens" (395 U.S. 367, 389). That there is no First Amendment right to have a license to broadcast also means, then, that one holding such a license has no constitutional right to hold it to the exclusion of his or her fellow citizens. There is certainly an implication in such an assertion that what a licensee may say in broadcasting is subject to some government control, notwithstanding the First Amendment. On the other hand, the high court did acknowledge that broadcasting is a medium "affected by a First Amendment interest" and cited section 326 of the Communications Act (which denies the commission censorship power). But the opinion offers no elucidation as to what First Amendment rights broadcasters may have in using the spectrum. The Court ultimately declared such rights (whatever they may be) inferior to those of both speakers-without-a-license and listeners. Broadcasters were put in a position analogous to that of trustees—fiduciaries, with obligations to protect the public's interest in the use made of the limited number of frequencies available to be licensed.

Because of the scarcity of radio frequencies, the government is permitted to put restraints on licensees in favor of others whose views should be expressed on this unique medium. But the people as a whole retain their interest in free speech by radio and their collective right to have the medium function consistently with the ends and purposes of the First Amendment. It is the right of the viewers and listeners, not the right of the broadcasters, that is paramount (395 U.S. 367, 390).

The fairness doctrine, the Court held, did not infringe broadcasters' First Amendment rights. More broadly, one might generalize from the opinion that the government may constitutionally impose restrictions on speech rights of its licensees under the Communications Act. Requirements of the fairness doctrine were simply the first of such possible restrictions to be identified.

The Court also dealt with two broadcaster objections (in addition to the constitutional one) to imposition of fairness doctrine obligations. The broadcasters argued that requiring licensees to devote time to coverage of issues and to reply rights for persons criticized would serve to inhibit the very coverage of the important issues the doctrine was intended to encourage. They also urged that any scarcity of frequencies that might have justified government regulation was a thing of the past.

Answering the first contention, the court noted the FCC's conclusion that broadcasters had been regularly providing coverage of public issues, so no "inhibition" problem appeared to exist. "If present licensees should suddenly prove timorous," continued the Court, "the commission is not powerless [to enforce its rules]."

With respect to the second contention, the Court asserted that there continue to be more persons who wish to broadcast than can be licensed to do so; therefore, comparative license proceedings are not a thing of the past. If the situation changes, the FCC or someone else may bring that change to the Court's attention and the current decision might then be reconsidered. In closing, however, the Court hinted that any optimism engendered by a possible reconsideration of the *Red Lion* holding should be tempered by the fact that "existing broadcasters have often attained their present position because of their initial government selection in competition with others before new technological advances opened new opportunities for further use" (395 U.S. 367, 400).

Licensees were thus put on notice that the Court recognized that the wealth and power the licensees had achieved was not solely a result of their entrepreneurial skills, but was also due in large measure simply to having been the successful license applicant in a comparative license proceeding.

Treatment by the Court of "scarcity" issues has been interpreted by opponents of government regulation of broadcasting as having included within the concept of "scarcity" all manner of media outlets. For example, in its 1985 report (which supported its 1987 decision to abandon the fairness doctrine), the commission claimed that there are great numbers of journals, newspapers, and CATV operations; therefore, the doctrine is no longer needed to keep the American people informed. Furthermore, there are enough operating broadcast frequencies to do the job without reference to other media. The facts have changed, the report concluded, as the Court had anticipated might happen. In sum, the commission study purported to demonstrate that the legal foundation for the fairness doctrine, as set forth in *Red Lion,* is no longer viable. Ergo, at least as of 1985, the doctrine unconstitutionally infringes the free speech rights of broadcasters.

Although the *Red Lion* opinion is ambiguous as to the importance to the Court's thinking of the quantity of information outlets other than broadcasting, I believe the Court's holding rests on the fact that the number of broadcasters who can be licensed is limited. If that understanding of the case is correct, the number of newspapers and magazines available at any given time would have no effect on the Court's decision.

In addition to treating all forms of information outlets as being fungible so far as the *Red Lion* holding is concerned, the commission's 1985 report ignores issues of single ownership of several outlets of one kind, or of single ownership of different kinds of such outlets. Both sorts of ownership are believed by many to pose serious threats to maintaining an informed public. (See, for example, Bagdikian 1994.) The commission ignored the Court's allusion to the fact of comparative license proceedings, making no attempt to show that such proceedings in broadcast license applications are "a thing of the past." Finally, the report simply ignores the Court's cautionary statement previously quoted.

It is fair to say, I think, that the legal status of the fairness doctrine remains unimpaired. Until changed by the Supreme Court, *Red Lion* continues to represent good law. But *Red Lion* upheld government power only to impose the fairness doctrine; it did not say the doctrine was required. There was every reason to believe the commission retained the right to decide to abandon the doctrine, and such an outlook has proved correct. So much for the current legal status of the fairness doctrine. Whereas issues relative to the doctrine are discussed in other chapters, my purpose in the remainder of this chapter is to examine some of the social and political aspects of the dispute between supporters and opposers of the doctrine.

In addition to the commission's opinion that the world of broadcasting had evolved since 1969 to the point that the fairness doctrine had come to violate broadcasters' First Amendment rights, the commission offered a second major justification for the decision to abandon the doctrine. The doctrine's purpose was to promote coverage of controversial issues of public importance. The commission's report concluded that, in operation, the doctrine had and has the opposite effect, in fact acting to *discourage* such coverage.

The report's reasoning begins with the fact that only once during its history has the FCC issued an order to a licensee requiring it to cover a controversial issue. The dearth of such actions, the report argues—and undoubtedly correctly so—has resulted from the inability of the commission to formulate a definition of "controversial issues" that broadcasters can use to identify matters they must cover. As a consequence, broadcasters can disregard this doctrinal obligation without fear of consequences. In fact, the consequences of such disregard have turned out to be beneficial to the licensee. If a station simply omits from programming any reference to matters that can be construed as "controversial issues of public concern," it need never fear attempts by outsiders to demand time for expression of another point of view, or for reply by someone who was allegedly criticized—two parts of the doctrine the commission *does* enforce. If the broadcaster avoids both of those possibilities, it avoids devoting time to uses that produce no revenue. For broadcasters, as for everyone else in the world, time is money!

Did the commission have any hard evidence that the doctrine discouraged coverage of controversial issues? It had letters from licensees affirming the correctness of the report's conclusion but lacking any real proof. That such evidence, without hard data, might be less than persuasive, if only because tainted by the obvious interest of the broadcasters in the doctrine's demise, was not mentioned in the report.

The strongest evidence supporting the commission's conclusion was "common sense." Who would freely give away valuable radio time, and thus money? That such a foolish giveaway might result from obedience to legal requirements the commission didn't discuss. The report also fails to indicate that the commission gave any consideration to possible modification of the doctrine short of outright abrogation. Perhaps exploring possibilities for making the doctrine more effective seemed irrelevant in light of the commissioners' views that it infringed broadcasters' First Amendment rights. Besides, such an undertaking would not have been consistent with the commission's ideological conviction that government regulation of broadcasting should yield before the efficient regulation of the "free market."

Dennis Patrick, under whose FCC chairmanship the fairness doctrine was ended, like his predecessor, Mark Fowler, was a devout free marketer. Many of those who opposed the doctrine opposed any government regulation of broadcasting. One such opponent, former University of Virginia professor Ronald A. Coase, had urged privatization of the spectrum. Coase wrote a number of law journal articles, among which is his oft-cited "The Federal Communications Commission" (1959)[1] in which he argues for such privatization. Coase believed courts, using common law doctrine, could solve signal interference problems, a view that has been generally discredited because the vagrant quality of electromagnetic signals requires an interstate, that is, national, solution. Even ardent free marketers concede the need for something like an FCC to police the spectrum.[2] A currently popular idea similar to the Coase approach is to auction rights in the spectrum. This would produce revenue from users of broadcasting privileges, many of whom have become fabulously wealthy because they were fortunate enough to have FCC licenses that cost them nothing—a scandalous fact in the minds of auction proponents. The idea has enough surface appeal to deserve closer examination, however.

The first difficulty of auctioning all spectrum rights is defining what would be sold. A license? And for what term? Could the license be subject to conditions beyond an expiration date? Could the term be renewed? If so, would there be a new auction? Might the "license" be permanent, like a "fee simple license"? Such concepts are not unheard of. Public bodies have "easements" to maintain streets. The rights end if the street is abandoned, so such title is not "fee simple," yet the public owner of the right

can determine by its actions when and if its possessory rights will terminate. Such questions remain unaddressed in the proposals to auction
broadcast rights.[3]

Assuming continuance of current practice, that is, sale of a license
with a fixed term, not sale of outright ownership of the frequency, auction
proposals seem to overlook the fact that the price the licensee was expected
to "pay" under the Communications Act was its obligation to serve the
public interest. Payment of sizable sums for use of frequencies, though perhaps sufficient even to retire a large chunk of the national debt, would also
provide potent ammunition for arguments against any contention that
users of the spectrum should have a duty to serve the public interest. If the
interest auctioned was a license subject to possible renewal or grant to another, what qualifications other than the amount to be paid could provide
a standard to determine the winner? In the absence of any definite gov-
ernment-imposed obligation to serve the public interest (meaning more
than such "obligations" resulting from the play of free markets and that
programs be on clear signals), perhaps broadcasters could be charged a fee
for spectrum use figured as a percentage of gross revenues derived from
broadcasting. Such fees might provide some minimal incentive for the
broadcaster to provide some unsponsored public-interest programming
just to reduce the annual fee. On the other hand, even programming concerning controversial issues could be quite biased, absent any requirement
for fullness and fairness.

The allegation of the 1985 report that FCC failure to enforce the first
part of the fairness doctrine, that broadcasters provide coverage of controversial issues, has worked to discourage such coverage is not an absurd
claim. Yet we know that there was coverage of such issues by licensees prior
to 1987, and that such coverage was significant. Also, if the FCC's failure
did operate to discourage issue coverage, it would be reasonable to think
that the commission anticipated such coverage would increase as a consequence of discarding the doctrine. No such increase is apparent. If there
have been any studies to demonstrate the results one way or the other, I am
not aware of them. Most possessors of wealth are conservative. Broadcasters are no exception, and so-called "talk" radio evidences a strong tendency
toward a sort of coverage of controversial issues loaded in favor of the rightness of the right. Is this the increase in coverage of controversial issues we
should have expected?

Legality of the commission's elimination of the doctrine was tested in
court, and the court of appeals for the District of Columbia upheld the
commission's action. The court did not have to consider the FCC con-

tention that the doctrine is unconstitutional, and it did not do so. It merely decided that under the Communications Act the commission has the discretionary power to terminate the doctrine, and no abuse of discretion was shown in its decision to do so.

As previously noted, the major foundation for the contention of the commission that the doctrine discourages discussion of controversial issues is the inability of the commission ever to produce a usable definition of "controversial issue"—a serious problem, though not fatal to actual broadcaster coverage of such issues. A similar definitional problem exists with respect to the word "obscene," which also eludes any precise definition. Yet we continue to make use of the word because of the importance the concept is thought to have for our society. Justice Potter Stewart's famous statement anent hard-core pornography, that he might not be able to define it, but he knows it when he sees it, seems to provide our fall-back position.

The justice's statement suggests a possible approach to the problem of defining "controversial issues." The doctrine could be expanded to add to broadcaster obligations a duty to make periodic announcements regarding the doctrine's requirements. So informed, listeners complaining about compliance failures might bring new life to the doctrine's use, at least enhancing the ability of broadcasters to recognize controversial issues when they see them. In any event, if the fairness doctrine has value, and I believe it does, the inability to define its coverage should not work to end it any more than the inability to define "obscene" leads us to throw up our hands and allow all "speech" to be protected by the Constitution. (Some might like this idea, but probably not simply because of the definitional difficulty.)

Finally, the commission's assumption of virtually total disregard by broadcasters of their obligations under the doctrine simply because they can "get away" with it—and profit from it in the bargain—is at least suspect as providing an acceptable rationale for government abrogation of an otherwise socially important regulation.

Notes

1. Another more recent work by DeVany et al. (1980) details an approach to privatization. Professor Lucas A. Powe Jr. once entertained similar ideas (1987). More recently he has concluded that regulation at the federal level is necessary to prevent signal interference because the promiscuous character of electromagnetic

waves, uncontrollable in crossing state lines, renders unworkable regulation by state courts applying common law concepts (the only alternative to federal regulation). See Krattenmaker and Powe 1994, 16-17.

2. See note 1, above.

3. It is current commission practice to auction rights in some parts of the spectrum. Those parts consist of wavelengths in the higher frequencies, useful for transmissions over very short distances. They include microwaves used for local TV relay, and facilities for cellular phones and CB transmissions. The rights auctioned consist of a license to use a specified frequency for a specified period. No permanent rights are sold: The licenses are always for a term, subject to renewal, regardless of the difficulty or ease of renewal.

CHAPTER 12

Money, Media, Politics, and Democracy

The role of money in politics today is of great concern to many people. It costs a lot of money to run for office. The higher the office sought, the greater the cost, and the cost in virtually every case has been going up at rates far exceeding that of inflation. Individual politicians seem to have little choice but to engage in the money-raising game if they are to have any hope of winning. Inevitably, sizable sums of money come from people who can afford to contribute generously. This raises questions of obligation. Is the successful politician obligated to serve the voters who put him or her in office, or the folks who financed the successful campaign? This is not a legal question, but a practical one. Should any politician be put in this position?

Raising money to finance election campaigns not only creates the problem of conflict of interest, it also takes a lot of time on the part of the office holder, who could otherwise spend it performing his or her job, or just thinking about the problems the job entails. One of the reasons running for public office is so expensive is broadcasting. The cost of radio and (particularly) TV time is very high. Bearing in mind that a great majority of Americans say they get most of their news from television, it is not surprising that candidates who receive minimal TV exposure generally occupy the ranks of the "also rans." No TV exposure, nobody knows who you are.

In 1971 Congress passed a voter reform law. The most important attempt at election reform in this century, it limited the amount of money a candidate could receive from any one contributor, and it limited the amount anyone not affiliated with a candidate could spend in support of election of that candidate. In *Buckley v. Valeo* 424 U.S. 1 (1976), the Supreme Court held the latter stipulation an unconstitutional infringement of speech. To limit the extent that a citizen can express views by limiting the amount that can be spent publicizing those views was held to violate one's First Amendment rights. The Court left standing limitations on the amount one donor could contribute to a candidate's campaign, but by removing the limit on expenditures supporters could independently spend, the Court rendered the act virtually meaningless, as Justice Byron White pointed out in his dissent. Ever since this decision, election reform has foundered on the shoals of the Court's view of the First Amendment as expressed in *Buckley*. If limiting spending is unconstitutional, how can the money race be eliminated?

There is currently before Congress the McCain/Feingold bill, which would mandate a certain amount of broadcasting time for candidates for federal office and award specified monetary benefits to candidates who voluntarily restrict their limitless pursuit of cash. But many people who have given consideration to the problem have concluded that there is no real hope of resolving the "money" problem short of either overruling *Buckley* or modifying the First Amendment. The unwillingness of Congress even to bring the McCain/Feingold bill to a vote shows the difficulty of legislating even an admittedly weak measure of change. The January-February 1998 issue of the *American Prospect* devoted considerable attention to the *Buckley* decision and the problem of money in politics. One argument for altering the Constitution was the fear of unanticipated consequences of a Court decision overruling *Buckley* in the absence of any change in the Constitution. Another argument considered *Buckley* a correct decision that should be left alone but also considered tampering with the First Amendment a dangerous approach to fine-tuning free speech protection. Perhaps there is another way.

The fairness doctrine requires coverage of controversial issues in a manner whereby all sides of an issue may be fairly represented. Part of the doctrine, identified as the Zapple doctrine, bridges a gap between the fairness doctrine and the terms of sections 312 and 315 of the Communications Act. These two sections, discussed in chapter 7, relate to the time made available to candidates, either for federal office or, under some circumstances, for *any* office.

When the counsel to the Senate Communications Subcommittee on Communications, Nicholas Zapple, inquired of the commission whether the fairness doctrine had any role in instances in which a spokesperson other than the candidate himself pitched the candidate's cause, the commission said yes. The resulting "Zapple" doctrine (as the FCC developed in 23 FCC2d 707 [1970] and 36 FCC 2d 40 [1972]) provides that appearance by a noncandidate in favor of a candidate triggers a right to have a noncandidate supporter appear on behalf of the other candidate(s). Time must be made available for a spokesperson for the other candidate on the same terms as the trigger event, including being charged the same fee if the triggering appearance had been bought. The commission considered whether the time to respond should be free, as in other applications of the "right of reply," but decided this could involve subsidization of a campaign, a result it found unacceptable. One commissioner, Nicholas Johnson, thought there might be circumstances under which such time *should* be provided free. The example the majority of commissioners cited in its contrary decision was that the chairperson of one of the two major parties speaks for its presidential candidate, triggering a right of response in the chairperson for the other major party. The time supplied to the second party should not, they thought, be "free."

Johnson believed the majority's cited example, and resulting conclusion, too limiting. Rather than emphasize possible subsidization of the national parties by broadcasters, he pointed to the importance of broadcasters' obligations to keep the public informed. Competition among party chairpersons was not the only conceivable scenario for use of the doctrine. Need for public education might, Johnson believed, outweigh the problems of campaign subsidization that concerned the majority.

The point of this exercise (some might say "fantasy") is that in restoration of the fairness doctrine and a new invigoration of the Zapple doctrine might be found a legal way around hurdles involved in either overruling *Valeo* or changing the First Amendment. The Supreme Court held that the fairness doctrine does not violate the First Amendment, and it could resolve many issues presented by so-called "issue" advertising, whereas its offshoot, the Zapple doctrine, might level the playing field in candidate races.

Congressional action would be required—a long shot in today's political climate. But political climates change, and such a course does not seem to present constitutional issues like those involved in *Valeo* or in the McCain/Feingold legislative effort.

CHAPTER 13

Must Broadcasters Be Licensed?

Broadcasting certainly involves "speech." Then why must one be licensed by the federal government to be a broadcaster? What justifies limiting broadcasters' First Amendment rights in a manner not applicable to print media? As I have pointed out in prior chapters, many opponents of government regulation of broadcasting interpret the *NBC* and *Red Lion* cases as holding that, because of spectrum scarcity, the license requirement for broadcasters does not infringe the First Amendment. They also seem to believe that, for the same reason, these cases determined First Amendment protections for broadcasters are inferior to those of, say, newspapers. This interpretation of these two cases is a distortion that has served to undermine the authority of the holdings in these cases and the intellectual integrity of the court's reasoning. These misinterpretations have led to muddled thinking, lumping together two separate issues—constitutional validity of licensing and constitutionality of government regulation of program content—as both having been upheld on the ground of scarcity.

The fact is that the litigants in both cases virtually stipulated to the constitutionality of the license requirement feature of the 1934 Communications Act if only by failing to contest that constitutionality. They also acknowledged in their briefs that broadcasting in the 1920s had led to chaos, necessitating the adoption of the Radio Act (predecessor to the Communications Act), which imposed order on the spectrum by authorizing the commission to determine who would be permitted to broadcast. The questions presented to the court in *NBC* and *Red Lion* were whether or not particular FCC actions infringed the First Amendment. In other words, whether FCC actions concerning licensee-programming, as opposed to licensing itself, infringe the First Amendment. The decisions of the Court in those cases held that the FCC rules did not infringe First

Amendment rights of persons licensed under the Communications Act.

The issue of "scarcity" is something of a red herring. Comparing newspaper ink and newsprint to frequencies is comparing apples with oranges. Frequencies are not "things" like ink and paper; limitations on the ability to communicate via wireless result from technical "deficiencies" in the ability of receivers to differentiate one signal from another. Except when one transmitter uses the same signal as another in the area served by both, signals don't "interfere" with each other. The "interference" we "hear" arises primarily from a "failure" of the receiving equipment. Licensing in broadcasting, as opposed to the printed press, can be justified by the nature of the spectrum and congressional concern with issues of monopoly relative to it. It also finds justification in the process of defining broadcast properties. In any case, licensing is unlikely to disappear as the system for choosing broadcasters, and the licensing system itself justifies lesser First Amendment rights for broadcasters as opposed to newspaper journalists.

Judicial Treatment of Licensing

As heretofore pointed out, no case ever required the Supreme Court to consider an argument that limiting broadcasting to government licensees violates the First Amendment. Any statements on the subject from the bench are, therefore, what lawyers call "dicta," or commentary that is not part of the holding of a case.

The three cases usually cited to support the proposition that such a judicial determination has been made are *Nelson Bros. Bond and Mortgage Co. v. FRC, NBC v. U.S.,* and *Red Lion Broadcasting Co., Inc. v. FCC.* In *Nelson Bros. Bond and Mortgage Co. v. FRC,* the plaintiff lost its broadcast license and questioned the FRC's power to cancel it. Noting that the license under which Nelson Bros. was operating was subject to revocation, the Court had little difficulty upholding the commission's power to cancel. The plaintiff never argued that its rights of free speech had been infringed by licensing. To do so would have been difficult because the broadcaster had accepted the benefits of licensing since 1925. Nor did Nelson Bros. contend that Congress lacked power to adopt the Radio Act. Describing the case presented to it by Nelson Bros., the Court said: "No question is presented as to the power of the Congress, in its regulation of interstate commerce, to regulate radio communications" (289 U.S. 266, 279). And later: "That the Congress has the power . . . to delete stations, in view of the limited radio facilities available and the confusion that would result from interferences, is not open to question" (289 U.S. 266, 282).

The first of these statements is at best ambiguous. It can be read either as simply describing the case presented, or as a statement of the Court's opinion. Because Nelson Bros. had literally not questioned such congressional power, the former seems the better choice. The second statement could be more credibly considered an expression of the Court's opinion but was made without there having been any contrary argument from the plaintiff, and without any First Amendment issue being raised. It, too, *can* be read as merely describing the factual setting of the dispute the Court was to resolve and is, therefore as ambiguous as the first statement. Yet both assertions became authority in *NBC* and *Red Lion* for the conclusion that there can be no question about Congress's power to license broadcasters under the commerce clause. There can be no question, that is, unless someone raises it, as Preferred Communications successfully did with respect to the "unquestionable power" of Los Angeles over use of its public rights-of-way, including installation of CATV delivery systems in *Preferred Communications, Inc. v. City of Los Angeles* 476 U.S. 488 (1985). But no one has questioned the power to license broadcasters.

The second of the three cases, *NBC v. FCC,* is discussed at length in chapter 7. In it NBC had sought to *limit* the scope of FCC power but not to "sink" the Communications Act. In addressing itself to NBC's position, the Court always assumed the validity of licensing. Not everyone, it said, can be licensed to broadcast. One might quibble about whether the fact that not everyone may be licensed refers to the nature of the spectrum or to the impact of the statute, or both, but "licensing" assumes the existence of the statute. The fact remains that no one attacked the licensing requirement of the statute as being unconstitutional, so the "quibble" was never addressed.

In the third case, *Red Lion Broadcasting Co., Inc. v. FCC,* the Court averred that there is no First Amendment right to broadcast, citing the *NBC* case as authority. As in the *NBC* case, no party in *Red Lion* claimed that the licensing system under the Communications Act is unconstitutional. So the Court's opinion in *Red Lion* assumes that the licensing system *is* valid, just as in the two other cases. Therefore any statement by the Court to the effect that licensing is valid in face of a First Amendment attack is dictum.

In spite of the foregoing, it is the general view that the licensing issue has been decided—that is, requiring a license to broadcast does not infringe First Amendment rights. Notwithstanding the weakness of the foundations for such an outlook, there is not much chance now that the Supreme Court will one day declare the licensing requirement unconstitutional. So let us now examine some contentions swirling around this nonexistent Supreme Court holding put forth by those who oppose the government regulation of broadcasting, and by those who support it.

Scarcity and Monopoly Concerns

The concept of "scarcity" was raised in the *NBC* decision when the Court described the spectrum as not available for use by everyone, suggesting that being scarce is its character and its limitation. But, apart from FCC licenses, what is supposedly "scarce"? Some say the answer to that question is "frequencies." But any attempt to reduce frequencies to a numerical value is like trying to determine how many waves there are in the ocean. What is scarce, then, appears to be the number of "channels" available for wireless transmission of signals detectable on a reliable basis by receivers. So viewed, the scarcity is not simply numerical but, some commentators claim, allocational (Carter 1994). Proponents of the latter consider that because of the spectrum's physical limits, the government is obliged to select those who will be licensed to broadcast from the large number of license-applicants. Allocational theory does not, though, seem capable of eliminating all "numerical" aspects of scarcity and thus fails to provide a satisfactory riposte to critics of the "scarcity" rationale as justifying broadcast regulation.

Such critics aver that all economic resources are scarce. Therefore, they assert that the scarcity rationale cannot justify the difference in treatment between broadcasters and newspaper publishers. Neither newsprint nor printer's ink is available in unlimited quantities. Yet, such critics say, this "scarcity" has never been thought to justify government regulation of newspapers or a governmental requirement that one have a license to publish a newspaper. It is true that newspapers are subject to some government regulation, including antitrust laws, zoning laws, civil rights laws, and many others, but these generally do not interfere with newspaper content. The editorial function is protected by the First Amendment (though there are limits even to that freedom).[1] Newspaper content is subject to much less government intrusion than is broadcasting. Critics insist that as the rationale for different treatment of print and electronic media, "scarcity" can't do the job.

Analogizing scarcity in the broadcast spectrum to a scarcity of newsprint in the world of journalism is troublesome because rolls of newsprint, unlike broadcast frequencies are material "things."[2] "Newsprint" may be thought of as supplying the "medium" for the newspaper just as the spectrum carries the broadcast, but that is not persuasive. For one thing, the number of rolls of newsprint will vary over time; the "number" of usable channels may increase, but it will never decline. The electromagnetic spectrum is not going to change, though our ability to use it might. A second problem with such analogy is that it implies a logical equivalency between newsprint relative to newspapers on the one hand, and broadcast frequencies to broadcasting on the other, an equivalency that is lacking because there are potential substitutes for newsprint in carrying the written word, whereas no such substitutes exist for frequencies in broadcasting. This points up the fact that while the supply of paper for carrying print is limited, it is, like many "scarce resources," in "plentiful" supply compared to some other "scarce resources," like broadcast frequencies. It becomes a matter of degree, a basis for according many matters different treatments. Last, comparison of rolls of newsprint to numbers of usable channels assumes that broadcast stations are fungible—that one is no different from another. From the beginning of licensing, availability of some stations produced considerable competition; others went begging. Channels at the low end of the spectrum are more desirable than those at the upper end. Broadcast channels are clearly not all equal, one interchangeable with another.

Michigan University Law School dean Lee Bollinger pointed out in his 1993 book, *Images of a Free Press*, that a major problem with the "scarcity" rationale for distinguishing the First Amendment treatment of broadcasting from the treatment of newspapers is the ambiguity surrounding that supposed rationale. As illustrated in the previous paragraph, pinning down a satisfactory meaning of scarcity in the broadcast context is an illusive business. Bollinger adds to the confusion, though, by concluding that the flawed nature of the widely accepted scarcity rationale was "unmasked" by Ronald Coase, "who pointed out the universality of scarcity."

The first critic of the so-called "scarcity" rationale seems to have been Leo Herzel, a University of Chicago law student who wrote a law review article urging the substitution of free market concepts for government regulation in allocating use rights in broadcasting. Herzel's thesis was cited by Ronald Coase in his 1959 article, "The Federal Communications Commission," one of two Coase articles Dean Bollinger refers to in his book, and the one in which Coase details his free market views. In the second article, in which he reiterates those views in more summary fashion, Coase writes: "But of course, as we all know, scarce resources are *normally* allocated in the United States by means of the pricing mechanism and a price emerges which is sufficiently high to reduce demand to equal the available supply" (Coase 1965, 161–62; emphasis added).

Unless Coase's use of the word "normally" was intended to be sarcastic, his statement implies that pricing in a free market is not the *only* means used in the United States for allocating scarce resources. Coase might claim that it *should* be the sole means for doing so, but I doubt he would. There are some things so important to life that their allocations are not left to the mercies of the market mechanism. There is government interference with the distribution of pharmaceuticals, in the distribution of medical care, and with respect to handling of body parts for human transplants. During wartime and other emergency situations the government resorts to rationing to ensure an equitable (politically determined) distribution of scarce resources, which could not be assured by reliance on the unhindered market. I would bet Coase would not have thought a shortage of wheat to be in the same category with a shortage of sand when considering whether distribution of these commodities, in short supply, should be left entirely to market operations.

Notwithstanding their devotion to free markets, most economists of that persuasion would, I believe, acknowledge that public utilities—"allocators" of water, energy, and some forms of transportation—should not be left solely to free market regulation. I assume Coase would agree with that view because reliance wholly on pricing would leave some members of society without these resources, presumably an unacceptable result for anyone. When, then, does a society look to markets as opposed to government for allocation of resources, all of which are supposedly scarce? Consideration of water resources in the western part of the United States, particularly in the states of the Southwest, reveals that the problem of selecting allocation techniques is more complex than might otherwise appear. Water availability in those states is a serious long-term issue. Regulated public utilities undertake allocation of currently available water relative to current need. Neither they nor the pricing mechanism would be able, unaided, to resolve long-range allocation issues; some more centralized government planning is essential. To leave such a problem to the utilities or to the market would be like leaving allocation of this resource, essential to life and also scarce, to throws of the dice, politically an unacceptable alternative for most people. And, I would judge, rightly so. Some effort at intelligent long-range planning for allocation of the limited water resources of the west must be attempted because of the *nature of the resource as well as its scarcity*.

In enacting the Communications Act, Congress was concerned with possible monopolization of that portion of the electromagnetic spectrum "available" for public use. Clarence Dill, primary author of both the 1927 Radio Act and the 1934 Communications Act, is quoted in the *NBC* case (319 U.S. 190, 221, note 5) as stating in the course of the 1927 Senate debate:

> As to creating a monopoly of radio in this country, let me say that this bill absolutely protects the public, so far as it can protect them, by giving the commission full power to refuse a license to anyone who it believes will not serve the public interest, convenience, or necessity. It specifically provides that any corporation guilty of monopoly shall not only not receive a license but that its license may be revoked; and if after a corporation has received its license for a period of three years it is then discovered and found to be guilty of monopoly, its license will be revoked. . . . Power must be lodged somewhere, and I myself am unwilling to assume in advance that the commission proposed to be created will be servile to the desires and demands of great corporations of this country.

Coase seems to have thought that antitrust laws could take care of all problems of monopolization. In fact, the antitrust laws would not necessarily address many aspects of monopolization of broadcast frequencies because such laws do not outlaw monopoly per se, but only unlawful acts undertaken for purposes of monopolization. Monopoly of the airwaves, legally achieved, would certainly be possible. Congressional concern to preempt such a possibility in an information distribution system considered important then, and on which today more than 90 percent of the adult population claims to depend for most of its news about the world, would be more justifiable than concern with preempting possible monopoly in, for example, my old friend, sand. Such preemptive action by Congress directed at broadcasting, but not at the printed press, does not present an obvious case of invidious discrimination. I can start a newspaper in New York City if I have the money to do so. Money or no, I cannot start a TV station today in that city and hope to have an audience, because of the license requirement, to be sure, but even in the absence of such requirement. Given this difference—a difference in degree, one might say—the congressional policy to prevent monopoly in the spectrum does not, I contend, unjustifiably subject broadcasters to antitrust controls in addition to those imposed by the Sherman and Clayton acts on *all* media, newspapers as well as broadcasting.

Krattenmaker and Powe are unsympathetic to the contention that broadcasters might be considered monopolists. They have argued that "one need not be an expert to know that the 'broadcasters are monopolists' position is demonstrably false. There is room in the spectrum for additional radio and television broadcasters. Television viewers can turn to newspapers, magazines, books, and radio for news and information [and elsewhere for entertainment]. . . . So long as Americans can read, think, and walk, broadcasters cannot be monopolists" (Krattenmaker and Powe 1994, 36).

These authors misconceive the thrust of the antitrust laws and the legal meaning of "monopoly." The market by which to determine the monopolistic status of a broadcaster is not necessarily the entire range of information sources. A single TV channel operator can be a monopolist. Each of us who has watched a TV program knows that, though armed with a mute, we will be compelled to watch each and every commercial if we want to be sure not to miss part of the program. The audience watches television for the program but constitutes a captive audience for the commercials, making the station licensee every bit as much a "gatekeeper" as cable operators were found to be in the *Turner Broadcasting System* case, in which the First Amendment rights of cable were diminished for the purpose of "saving free TV."

Additional evidence in support of the proposition that broadcasters are possessed of monopolistic characteristics in a way unlike newspapers can be found in the fact that anyone can subscribe to each and every newspaper and magazine published in the country. The same cannot be said with respect to receiving every broadcast transmission made.

Interstate Circuit v. U.S. 306 U.S. 208 (1939), in which the Justice Department successfully prosecuted major motion picture producers for violations of the antitrust laws, involved a market composed of first-run movie theaters; from which Americans surely could have walked away; on which surely Americans were not dependent for entertainment.

Recognition of a legitimate government concern with monopoly in the limited possible uses for broadcasting provides at least one justification for government choosing the users rather than leaving such choice to operation of the free market. I believe another justification can be found in the only practicable means for providing a definition for "broadcast properties," an undertaking viewed by Coase and others as essential for successful operation of a free market in such properties. I now turn to consideration of that matter.

Defining Property Interests in Broadcasting

Another basis for distinguishing between the broadcasting and print media arises from the regulatory critics' recognition that a property definition for broadcasting is a sine qua non for successful operation of a free market in broadcast rights. It might be argued that the market's need for such a definition carries within it the seeds of the unavoidable failure of the market to be able to cope with broadcasting free of government regulation.

Definition of a property interest in newspapers doesn't appear essential to the ability to publish one, or to the existence of a free market in their purchase and sale. Yet Coase, Krattenmaker and Powe, and others have contended that definitions of the property interests in broadcast frequencies are required for such a market in broadcast properties. Once such definitions are provided, government can be eliminated from any further regulatory function. This idea perhaps first appeared in Coase's 1959 article, "The Federal Communications Commission," wherein, comparing the FCC to an imaginary agency set up to license newspaper publications, Coase writes: "The situation in the American broadcasting industry is not essentially different in character from that which would be found if a commission appointed by the federal government had the task of selecting those who were to be allowed to publish newspapers and periodicals in each city, town, and village of the United States. A proposal to do this would, of course, be rejected out of hand as inconsistent with the doctrine of freedom of the press."

Pointing out that in the *NBC* opinion Justice Frankfurter described radio's facilities as limited, Coase asks why this justifies government choosing those to be permitted to broadcast. Even if facilities are limited, shouldn't the commission be regarded "as a kind of traffic officer, policing the wave lengths to prevent" interstation signal interference? The Court's response, as described by Coase, is that the statute does not so restrict the commission; rather, it places the job of broadcaster selection in government hands. This dialogue is presented by Coase in such a manner as to imply that the Court was making a policy decision that the Communications Commission *should* have the selection responsibility, when in fact the Court was simply reciting the statutory requirement. Perhaps this is an unintended misrepresentation. But Coase thereby raises the issue he wants to raise: Is government selection the only means for choosing broadcast licensees? He thinks not and recites the well-known story that before adoption of the Radio Act, predecessor to the 1934 act, broadcasting had descended into chaos. He quotes Professor Charles A. Siepmann as alleging that "private enterprise over seven long years [1920–27] failed to set its house in order. Cutthroat competition at once retarded radio's orderly development and subjected listeners to intolerable strain and inconvenience" (Coase 1959, 13).

These views and conclusions of Siepmann's, like those contained in the *NBC* opinion, were, says Coase, "based on a misunderstanding of the nature of the problem." Justice Frankfurter was wrong in believing that scarcity of frequencies required government selection of users. Siepmann was wrong in ascribing the seven years of chaos to a failure of private enterprise and the competitive system. The real cause of the trouble, claims Coase, "was that no property rights were created in these scarce frequencies. . . . A private-enterprise system cannot function properly unless property rights are created in resources, and, when this is done, someone wishing to use a resource has to pay the owner to obtain it. Chaos disappears; and so does government *except that a legal system to define property rights and to arbitrate disputes is, of course, necessary*" (Coase 1959, 14; emphasis added).

Once the property rights are defined, Coase concludes, allocation of those rights in broadcast frequencies should be accomplished by use of the pricing mechanism operating in a free market. Although Coase acknowledges that problems of monopoly might exist, he seems to believe our antitrust laws can deal with them. He never considers the kinds of monopoly concerns discussed in the previous section.

This asserted need for defining property rights, and the subsequent sale of such rights by the "owner," raises some preliminary questions. First, who is the "owner" from whom these property rights are to be purchased? If the answer is the U.S. government, why is there any need for further justification of a difference in treatment between newspapers and broadcasting so far as licensing is concerned? The government may dispose of its property as it sees fit. If the government is not the owner, it is difficult to conceive who is, and by what right it sells unspecified property interests in the electromagnetic spectrum. Let us assume, though, that such critics would acknowledge government to be the owner, yet urge that under First Amendment "principles" government "ought" to divest itself of such ownership. Before analyzing the possibilities of such an approach, we should note that if government *is* the acknowledged owner of the spectrum (even if only by default) a difference between the press and broadcasting has been identified sufficient to justify the difference in treatment accorded each. But now let's examine the divestment suggestion as a means for ending government role in broadcast regulation. Achieving the goal may not be so simple even were there general agreement on its desirability.

Apparently blind to the foregoing considerations, Coase proceeds to compare frequencies to land, analogizing the need for property definitions in the former with the fact of such definitions in the latter. But where are the property definitions in broadcasting to come from? The government, whether or not it is the "owner"? Was there chaos in the use of land before government provided definitions of property rights in land? Whatever the ancient origin of courts and even earlier methods of resolving disputes, property definitions in land did not, I suggest, spring from the minds of a national legislature. I have never heard it suggested with respect to any society in the Western world that all its land was ever owned by the sovereign or the state. Was Congress or the FCC needed to define property in frequencies? Coase (or a disciple) may waffle in his answer, though Coase mentions courts as needed to "define" property interests in frequencies and more confidently claims courts had even begun that process by applying common law principles to the resolution of signal interference problems, citing *Tribune Co. v. Oak Leaves Broadcasting Station* (Cir. Ct., Cook County, Ill., 1926; reproduced in 68 Cong. Rec. 216, 1926). This must mean that in his judgment no government action is absolutely essential (though perhaps convenient) for the defining of the needed property interests. Citation of the Cook County case with the significance attached to it by Coase has the unfortunate consequence, for Coase's thesis, of undermining his dismissal of Professor Siepmann's critique of free enterprise. If common law definitions can provide broadcasters with the armor of a property definition needed to protect their rights, why is Siepmann's critique of free market performance incorrect?

A difficulty in defining a property right in broadcasting is presented by the fact that any such definition must take account of a certain dynamic aspect in spectrum use. Important purposes that the definition must serve are prevention of interference by one such "property-owner" with signals of another, and prevention of interference by any and all such property owners with legitimate activities of private persons. Insofar as prevention is dependent on the state of a broadcaster's equipment, the definition must impose an ongoing obligation to keep broadcast equipment in condition adequate to the tasks. Broadcasting operations may be said to be in a state of continuous "tension" to avoid interference of the kinds identified, necessitating periodic inspection and testing of that equipment to be sure performance standards are met.

In light of such considerations, it is difficult to conceive of a source for such definitions other than the federal government, the source of such definitions today. If broadcast rights as so defined were then auctioned off to private users, free market advocates see government's role in broadcasting as ending, *except*, as Coase notes, that "a legal system to arbitrate disputes is, of course, necessary." The task of settling disputes arising from gaps in the definitions and other disagreements among broadcasters, and between broadcasters and nonbroadcasters, would presumably fall to the courts, but which courts? Coase assumes the common law would supply the applicable legal framework. State courts are the primary users of the common law. Because electromagnetic signals are both vagrant, crossing state lines unpredictably, and *intended* to cross state lines, no single state's courts would have sufficient jurisdiction to handle such matters. Krattenmaker and Powe recognize this difficulty and suggest that a federal common law could deal with the problem (Krattenmanker and Powe 1994, 17). In 1936, however, in *Erie Railroad Co. v. Tompkins* (308 U.S. 64), a personal injury case, the Supreme Court held that the Constitution admits of no federal common law; federal courts are required, the Court said, to apply the common law of the state where the federal court is located when use of common law is required. The holding in that case related to tort law, generally thought to be beyond the scope of federal power under the commerce clause. Conceivably, federal common law dealing with broadcasting could be fashioned, but that it could be done constitutionally by the judiciary is highly doubtful; it would take an act of Congress, making the federal government once again the major player. But we already have the Communications Act. In the end it might be easier simply to leave the FCC in existence as the required dispute resolution agency. This would be particularly sensible in light of the definitional difficulties previously noted, and given the existence of an FCC staff with extensive technical expertise.

In theory the FCC's functions could be limited simply to providing dispute resolution of the previously described type for the benefit of broadcasters whose operations are otherwise out of bounds so far as government interference is concerned. Whether a tax-financed agency that provides dispute resolution for wealthy private station owners who wish to protect their monopoly status with respect to the frequencies they "own" would be politically acceptable, even if legal, is another question. Aside from that, such an arrangement suggests another possible justification for limiting broadcasters' First Amendment rights, that is, their status as beneficiaries of federal largesse, which, under *Rust v. Sullivan* 500 U.S. 173 (1991), could justify government control over aspects of their speech. In *Rust* the

Court held that the First Amendment does not bar government imposition of speech restrictions on family-planning clinics (and those working for them, including M.D.'s) that receive some federal funding—a position some might argue broadcasters already occupy, as a matter of fact.

Two major theories to justify placing broadcasters in a position protected by lesser First Amendment rights than the printed press (and two other possible grounds, suggestive though not developed) have now been examined, that is, scarcity in combination with monopoly concerns, and the peculiar position of the electromagnetic spectrum relative to the apparent need to define broadcast "property rights." Neither theory has been subjected to judicial evaluation. If in some manner that could be done, do we have any indication as to how the Supreme Court might proceed? In 1968 the high court did decide a nonbroadcasting case, and its approach may provide a clue. In that case, *O'Brien v. U.S.* (also discussed in chapter 10), a young man burned his draft card in public to protest the war in Vietnam. The Selective Service Act forbade mutilation of the draft card, and O'Brien was prosecuted and convicted of violating that law. His defense was that his action was "speech" protected by the First Amendment, a defense the trial court rejected. The Supreme Court upheld O'Brien's conviction even on his theory that his act was "speech," and in doing so enunciated a rule for determining the constitutionality of government acts that indirectly restrict speech.

Such government acts would not offend the First Amendment, the Court said, if (a) they were in furtherance of a legitimate and substantial government interest, (b) they were not specifically directed at speech, and (c) they operated to limit speech as little as possible while still accomplishing the government's purpose. This rule of the *O'Brien* case was not particularly novel; basically, it encapsulated results of earlier Supreme Court decisions. It was unique primarily in its inductive generalization.

Had the court in *NBC* been faced with an argument as to whether the government *had* to choose which of a number of applicants was to be selected to be *the* broadcaster *because* it was important that *someone* be heard, it might well have used something like the *O'Brien* rule in its analysis. Was it an important and legitimate government interest *to be sure that someone was heard* on each available channel? Was the licensing system to accomplish this the least intrusive means with respect to First Amendment rights? The short answer to both questions is that the case was neither presented to the Court nor analyzed by it in those terms.

Some might be alarmed that such a rule might be used today in a case dealing with the printed press. That is extremely unlikely for two reasons.

First, the rule itself limits its application to government acts *not* specifically directed at speech; the statute in *Tornillo v. Miami Herald* (discussed in chapter 7) was specifically directed at speech. Second, the Court has developed three general approaches to First Amendment cases. Deciding which approach to take in a suit involves a preliminary determination by the court as to whether the case presents a question requiring strict scrutiny, intermediate scrutiny, or a lesser scrutiny, the last identified with the *Red Lion* approach. How the Court decides on the proper approach is beyond the scope of this book. *Tornillo*, though, provides the model for the strict scrutiny approach, placing print media in the "preferred" position. The intermediate scrutiny is that of *O'Brien*. If *Red Lion* signifies the third approach, how could the Court utilize the stricter *O'Brien*-type test in a broadcasting case? Two answers: *Red Lion* dealt with the fairness doctrine *within* the context of licensing, whereas our hypothetical future case would be testing the constitutionality of licensing itself. Second, the Court's three-standard rule for deciding speech cases had not yet been conceived, and no party in *Red Lion*, much less *NBC*, argued for use of the rule of the *O'Brien* case. *Red Lion* having been decided, and the decision having rested on the fact of licensing, it is probably idle to speculate on the Court's consideration of a case questioning the constitutionality of licensing. However, suggesting a possible approach may serve to clarify some of the issues involved.

Virtually all critics of government regulation of broadcasting cite the seemingly strange fact that broadcasters are permitted to use this valuable resource without paying anything. Coase goes so far as to allege that use of a pricing mechanism was "completely unfamiliar to most of those concerned with broadcasting policy" (Coase 1959, 17). In this I think he is probably wrong. These were sophisticated businesspeople, familiar with market operations; they were not country rubes. The legislative idea was to demand public service from licensees. Whether the authors of the Radio Act gave thought to requiring financial compensation for use of the spectrum, I don't know. Because many licensees were nonprofits, schools and churches, the idea of charging a fee may have been dismissed as impractical. None of the commercial licensees rose to volunteer payment. That is neither strange, nor likely attributable to a "Gee, we never thought of that!" attitude, which Coase apparently believed to be the case.

There seems no insuperable obstacle to government charging a license fee from broadcasters so long as it does not compromise the requirement that broadcasting serve the public interest, as that concept was understood in years prior to the 1980s. In fact, a fee calculated as a percentage of the station's gross revenues might serve as an inducement to greater public interest coverage, coverage unlikely to attract much revenue and so reducing the license fee payable to the government.

Full First Amendment Protection for Broadcasters as Policy

Some critics of the current regulatory scheme seem to suggest that, legalities aside, as a policy matter broadcasters should be treated as though they enjoy the same First Amendment rights as print journalists because both perform similar functions[3]. Why not?

Virtually all Americans value the First Amendment and the right to be free of government regulation of speech. Formulating a political justification for free speech has been more difficult. An important objective is encouragement of the journalistic "flashlight," probing into official misconduct to preserve the integrity of the system. Another purpose may be seen in healthy ventilation; it's better to be able to "sound off" than not. There is also the conceit that free speech will lead to the prevalence of "truth" over "error"—to the extent we can know which is which. Perhaps the most important positive reason is to keep the citizenry informed. Journalistic exercise of free speech has often required considerable courage, notwithstanding existence of the First Amendment. Government pressures, social pressures, considerations of job responsibilities, and one's well-being can all be factors in deciding whether to speak about some things. Journalists are faced with many influences that can inhibit journalistic honesty and excellence. The First Amendment eliminates at least one major obstacle to uninhibited discussion of public issues—*impediments imposed by government.* If broadcasters were swept under the umbrella of First Amendment protection, would they start from the same position as their counterparts in print media? So long as the right to broadcast is subject to government licensing, the answer seems clearly no.

There is inherent in licensing some aspect of "chilling" of speech, itself a form of censorship. CBS newsman Richard Salant recognized its presence when, having interviewed Nikita Kruschev in 1957, he was questioned by government agents. We TV reporters are on the spot, Salant said, and added, "No matter what the law may say about immunity from censorship and about our guarantees of the First Amendment, there is always the brooding omnipresence that a broadcaster is a licensee and if he is not a licensee, he cannot be a broadcaster."

This statement, quoted by Professor Harry Kalven (then professor of law at the University of Chicago) in "Broadcasting, Public Policy, and the First Amendment" (1967), is described by Kalven as raising "the dismal question whether in a practical world the brute fact of the license spoiled the game." A city ordinance requiring a license for placement of newspaper vending machines was struck down by the Supreme Court in *City of Lakewood v. Plain Dealer Publishing Co.* 486 U.S. 750 (1980) as infringing the First Amendment because it created a similar chill. The ordinance, said the Court, made *"post hoc* rationalizations by the licensing official and the use of shifting or illegitimate criteria . . . far too easy," preventing reviewing courts from detecting abuse of power that could be used "to intimidate parties into censoring their own speech" (486 U.S. 750, 757–58).

Salant did not say his reporting had been chilled by the fact he worked for a licensee. Apparently unaware of any chilling effect until after the interview, he probably had not been intimidated. But he subsequently saw, and *articulated,* the existence of the chill. A problem for those served by broadcast journalism is that they are unaware whether the journalistic quality of what they hear has, or has not, been affected by such chill.

Anyone who thinks the 1996 Telecommunications Act reduced the chill factor doesn't understand it. The chill is a consequence of being a licensee; nothing indicates there is any current intent by Congress to alter that status, or by anyone to seek judicial reevaluation of the constitutionality of broadcast licensing. The chill factor might be said to be more in my head than in broadcasting. Is Rush Limbaugh chilled? Limbaugh's apparently sincere line is not seriously opposed to the political establishment, nor contrary to the interests of those who pay him. Nonetheless, the question betrays misunderstanding of the chill factor. How do we know Limbaugh is *not* "chilled" by reason of working for a licensee? In the *City of Lakewood* case, the Court was able to solve the problem of the chill by *eliminating its source,* invalidating the license requirement, *an option apparently not open with respect to broadcasters.* It might be argued that license renewal is pro forma, renewal seldom denied, virtually never in recent years, and the Telecommunications Act made renewal even easier. We are approaching the "fee simple" license. Nonetheless, to paraphrase the Supreme Court in *Red Lion,* license renewal is not yet a thing of the past. It is noteworthy, too, that denial of renewal in the past was at times grounded on claimed violation of technical FCC rules, though in fact denial was due to program content.[4] The Telecommunications Act, embodying the most recent trends toward relaxed regulation, did not eliminate licensing. Nor is that statute part of the Constitution. Despite the relaxed atmosphere, the Telecommunications Act remains an act of Congress. What Congress grants Congress can take away.

One objective of a free press is to produce open and robust debate, the better to keep the public informed. Print media enjoy full First Amendment protection *as a matter of constitutional law*. Extension of such protection to licensee broadcasters as a policy matter would be deceptive if it fooled listeners into believing broadcast journalism was conducted under the same rules and pressures as apply in print media. As long as broadcasters are licensees, they face at least one hurdle to robust and uninhibited coverage of the news that print journalists do not face—a hurdle that renders their performance virtually impossible of public evaluation, yet always open to question in a way print journalism is not. That the majority of viewers may be unaware of this "chilling" factor in broadcast journalism increases its danger, given that so many people depend on TV for most of their news.

So long as broadcasters are licensees of the government, their journalistic function is not performed under the same rules that apply to print; relative to speech, the operational environments of the two media are different.

Finally, if advocates of such a policy prevailed, their success would likely be reflected in congressional legislation prohibiting government from interfering with broadcast speech. Though perhaps successful in ending FCC regulation of program content, such a statute would almost certainly not affect action by state governments. If it did, Congress would have discovered a way to amend the Constitution without need of state ratification.

Either the printed press and broadcasters are possessed of the same First Amendment protections, or they are not; a game of "Let's pretend they are" is a charade.

Notes

1. Obscene material is not protected by the First Amendment, even in print; nor would effective urging of criminal activity be likely to escape official sanction.

2. A frequency is a mathematical construct relative to electromagnetic waves. Use of the word "channels" would probably be more exact in discussing "scarcity" issues. However, broadcast licenses are designated as identifiable parts of a frequency, so I use the two words more or less interchangeably.

3. Krattenmaker and Powe (1994) appear to so advocate in the last two chapters of *Regulating Broadcast Programming.*

4. In 1978 a license in the name of the University of Pennsylvania was denied renewal following complaints by neighbors about student language used in programs. The renewal-denial was grounded in the licensee's loss of control of the station as evidenced by the programs (*Trustees of the U. of Pennsylvania* 69 FCC2d 1394).

CHAPTER 14

Deregulation of Broadcasting

D
ismantling the regulatory scheme governing broadcasting, which began in the mid 1970s, continues to the present day. It is part of a larger movement freeing much of the economy from government regulation. Three arguments have been advanced to justify deregulation. A general argument, but applicable to broadcasting, is that the process of regulation has been taken over by the regulated; the only way to rid regulation of that cancer will be to root out the regulation. One argument specifically relating to broadcasting is that regulation interferes with broadcasters' rights, First Amendment and perhaps other. In this view government is considered bureaucratic (read "rigid"), and unfettered markets are thought to be the most efficient way to accommodate the wishes of the listening public. A second argument directed at broadcasting is that broadcasting is simply too complex for effective regulation by any government body, especially in light of the financial limits on an agency like the FCC. The workload the FCC currently faces, let alone long-range problems now visible, is simply too great for effective handling, and an increase in the FCC's resources does not loom on the horizon. Too often what requires disinterested and careful analysis is decided on the basis of political expediency—or so the thinking under the third rationale would have it.

A number of academics have spoken on questions of the future of broadcasting and the proper regulatory role, if any, of government. The most persistent and successful voices have come from devotees of free market thinking like Professors Lucas A. Powe Jr. and Thomas G. Krattenmaker. They jointly authored *Regulating Broadcast Programming* (1994); Powe alone wrote *American Broadcasting and the First Amendment* (1987). Their attack has been primarily aimed at the perceived justifications for government regulation suggested in the *NBC* and *Red Lion* cases. Expanding upon many of the positions enunciated by former judge Robert Bork, these two scholars have been successful in discrediting much of the reasoning of the two cited cases, largely because their assertions about those two cases have been uncritically accepted. The success of their arguments is partly due to the closeness of their positions to views of University of Chicago economists whose school of thought espouses all-out laissez-faire capitalism as expounded by Friedrich Hayek in *The Road to Serfdom* (1944) and elaborated upon by Milton Friedman and others such as Richard Posner and, more recently, Richard Epstein. Both Ronald Reagan and former British prime minister Margaret Thatcher were strongly influenced by the ideas these men voiced.

Friedman, Epstein, and Posner are, or were, teachers at the university level. One wonders if they conducted their classes in the manner they advocate society as a whole should be conducted. The students, as consumers, would know what they wanted, and the instructors would be obligated to meet their expectations. Or did these men consider that they knew better than the students what their courses should cover?

Education in general has been described as the process by which the wisdom (if any), the culture, and the thought of the past are handed down from generation to generation. The product is made up of ideas, convictions, "products" of the minds of millions. Why should not the teaching process also be governed by market concepts? Does not dictation by Epstein or Posner as to what material a course should cover interfere with the students' wants and desires? To assert that such "dictation" does not represent such a conflict because no one need attend Harvard, or Chicago, or wherever, and that choosing to do so is to accept the product there offered on the terms of the offer is, first, to beg the question, and second, to fail to be a thoroughgoing free marketer. Why may not the student body of Chicago decide that the makeup of a particular course is not to its liking? If enough of them decide to avoid that course, it might just disappear from the curriculum. To whose loss? The responses of free marketers and those not so enthralled might differ.

What makes the role of student consumers as deciders of course content an improper one, while the role of the TV viewer to watch soaps in every free TV hour is proper? Is the students' judgment as to the importance of a course less valuable than that of the instructor's? You bet it is. When dealing with ideas, with information, at least of certain types, some judgments are better than others, and my perceived wish to satisfy my needs may be faulty to the point that interference with my judgment may be appropriate. Does education, the passing on from generation to generation of the knowledge of the past, stop at the schoolhouse door?

In the world of book publishing for young people (for anyone, for that matter), is the conceivable preference of the target readers for comic books to be determinative of what is to be published, without interference? Ah, but these young are so—just that—"young." But at what age does the change to total market freedom take place? Is it to be the same for all? Harvard and Chicago (notwithstanding the "Chicago school") might be able to be selective and retain their positions of academic "excellence." What of state-supported schools? Are the land grant schools in the same position? Ought they to be?

Broadcasting, insofar as it deals with entertainment (difficult as that is to define) may be in the same boat with lipstick. Let the market decide which brand and shade will prevail. But with respect to information and news (also difficult to define), should a majority vote decide what the programming will be? Free market advocates would probably charge the originator of such thoughts with being Chicken Little. Plenty of journals are available to keep us informed. Public broadcasting also can still be seen on the tube, etc., etc. For how long? Congress came close to defunding public broadcasting in 1997. Increasingly, public broadcasting finds it necessary to turn to the business community for financial support. The further it proceeds along this line, the less difference there will be between "public" broadcasting and commercial broadcasting. To motivate public contributions, PBS asks, "If PBS doesn't do it, who will?" The unspoken assertion is that if PBS chooses *not* to do it or is unable to do it, it won't get done because no one competes with PBS to bring you such programming. That robust, investigative journalism has been seriously compromised as a result of deregulation of broadcasting seems a truism.

As for publishing, the free marketers' claim that there are ample publishers may be true, but as the information "business" increasingly yields to free market pressure, how long will it be true? The publishing world is more and more composed of corporations that are subsidiaries of other media entities, in turn usually owned by some larger corporation, often multinational in nature.

It has been noted that the broadcasting world, though it may ventilate criticism of particular journalists or spokespersons, has never provided serious discussion of the pros and cons of government regulation of the broadcast medium itself. Steve Weinberg pointed out that Congressman Van Deerlin's 1978 attempt to rewrite the Communications Act failed in no small measure because broadcasters, satisfied with the status quo, gave it zero coverage (Weinberg 1983). No interest in the proposal was shown by the public: How could it have been, when people were unaware of its existence? One need not be a devotee of conspiracy theories to understand that journalists, like other human beings, can judge where their interests lie, and what risks are and are not prudent, given the desire to continue to eat and feed the family. Nor does one have to be possessed of such theories to understand that wealthy media corporations often share outlooks common to corporations in many different fields, a result of their status, not of any "agreements." It takes no great brain to understand one does not bite the hand that feeds—or that one incurs great risk by doing so. It has always taken courage to be a dissident. It is easier if the dissident has a fallback position. Media monopolies tend to deny journalists such a position—and communicate that denial to those who make their living in the media.

Do we conceive that commercial broadcasting satisfies the listeners' "real" desires in programming, whereas public broadcasting provides some combination of both what the broadcaster determines "should" be covered, and what listeners acknowledge they ought to know, like taking an unpleasant medicine? How many of us really wanted to be "escorted" through the labyrinths of the Telecommunications Act before it was passed? Did we conceive there might have been another side to the criticisms of the Clinton administration's first-term health plan as voiced by "Harry and Louise" of TV fame? How many want to be told we may face nuclear disasters because of failure to clean up the nuclear waste site at Hanford, Washington, or because of a rusting fleet of subs of the former Soviet navy that may have nuclear components aboard? How can we analyze and act upon problems of possession of nuclear devices by so-called rogue states when such possession arises not from sale of the bombs by Russia or Ukraine, but because former "Soviet" nuclear physicists, whom neither Russia nor Ukraine can compensate adequately, have found that "rogue" states will pay them well?

Commercial broadcasting has largely ignored problems relative to global warming except to note that some scientists question the idea. Even less consideration has been given to possible human contribution to this phenomenon. Public broadcasting has done better, but not much. One result is that many of us are left skeptical as to whether there's really a problem at all. Some deprecate the whole idea, particularly when encountering an unexpected cold snap. Consideration of possible human contribution to problems of global warming opens another can of worms. The list of items broadcasting either trivializes or ignores goes on. What network gave serious coverage to Y2K problems?

Those who think we should know such things may (perhaps reluctantly) want such information. Those lacking any knowledge about such matters are unable to make an intelligent choice one way or the other. If we believe a full range of important information should be imparted to us, how is this to be accomplished if the market is to determine our broadcast fare?

The comparison of broadcasting's educational role to that of schools' cannot be pushed too far. Broadcasting companies are not staffed with professional educators, nor is broadcasting possessed of specific educational goals—other than the general one of helping (with other media) to keep the public "informed." The metaphor likening electronic media to formal institutions of learning is intended to underline the weaknesses of reliance on market operations to realize the educational function of broadcasting. Market operations require an assist if they are to fulfill broadcasting's educational role. The fairness doctrine provided such an assist.

When the FCC abandoned the fairness doctrine in 1987, it justified doing so with essentially two arguments: The doctrine violates First Amendment rights of broadcasters, and the doctrine discourages rather than encourages coverage of controversial issues. As discussed in chapter 11, the first reason incorrectly states the law, because the Supreme Court decided to the contrary in the *Red Lion* case and declined to reexamine that conclusion in its decision as recently as 1994 in *Turner* I (114 S. Ct. 2445 [1994]). Critics of *Red Lion* may consider both decisions to be wrong, or to "have become" wrong. They are free to do so. The commission, as part of the federal government, is not free to act on such a conclusion. The constitutionality of the doctrine was upheld. The decision has not been reversed. Under our system of government, agencies of the federal government are not at liberty to take actions based on their view that Supreme Court decisions are incorrect. In 1987 the commission did just that, but it "got away with it" because its action also qualified as a policy decision within its discretion.

Because the legal question is presently closed, the policy issue is of paramount importance. In saying the doctrine discouraged coverage of controversial issues rather than encouraged such coverage, the commission used language similar to that used by the Supreme Court itself in *Miami Herald v. Tornillo*, contending that robust debate would be inhibited by a state law requiring newspapers to cover the pros and cons of political candidates. The Court invalidated such a law. When made to the Supreme Court in *Red Lion* five years before *Tornillo*, that argument failed to sway the Justices—at least it didn't carry the day.

To kill the doctrine for its failure to encourage broadcaster coverage of controversial issues at least suggests that the commission believed the end of the doctrine would lead to an increase in such coverage. I have not heard of any studies either confirming or refuting whether that has happened. I doubt it has. Coverage of controversial issues seems currently supplied by talking heads, virtually all outrageously right-wing, and with no pretense of presenting another side in opposition to the revealed truth possessed by the radio or TV personality. Although the commission's conclusion that the fairness doctrine discouraged coverage of controversial issues may in some measure be correct, such coverage sometimes did take place, and it was many-sided. Absence of the doctrine seems to have made matters worse, not better. I have referred to a number of subjects that have been almost totally ignored by the electronic media since 1987. Whether those or comparable issues were better covered before that date, only time-consuming research might reveal, but certainly elimination of the doctrine has not resulted in increased coverage of such or like issues.

It might be contended that compulsory coverage of anything by free people using the airwaves is simply undemocratic. It therefore is unacceptable and should not be tolerated, no matter what its benefit. Besides, where is the governmental agency so bright and so trustworthy that it can safely be charged with the job of telling broadcast licensees what issues they should and should not cover, not to mention whether the coverage has been "thorough" enough?

Issues so raised are not simple. Similar questions have haunted the human race over centuries. One means of encouraging dissemination of the wide-ranging selection of information "needed" by a self-governing citizenry is to adopt limitations on common ownership of broadcast outlets. The object would be to have many editors independently select and produce broadcast programming. Widespread ownership of stations was an early and enduring goal of the FCC, but it has not been realized and was pretty much abandoned in enactment of the 1996 Telecommunications Act, with elimination of most of the limitations previously adopted by the commission.

In terms of shaping the performance of the media, the question, Who is in control? is an important one in our society.

> The media giants are . . . at the very heart of economic power—with a handful of companies dominating the main flow of information and entertainment. Their political and economic interests are not demonstrably different in general from those of General Motors, EXXON, USX, or DuPont. Their two principal sources of income are from advertising,

designed and paid for by the latter, and from the major political parties and their candidates.

Does this suggest a conspiracy to shape opinion and polls and politics and society? Doubtless such a conspiracy could be arranged, were it seen as necessary. It does not seem to be necessary. There is instead an "innocent" confluence of interests as when tiny streams pulled by gravity ultimately form a great river. (Dowd 1997, 26-27)

The First Amendment had its genesis providing protection from the habit of the all-powerful state to control what it conceived to be threats—spoken or written—to its status. There was no social entity then existing that rivaled the state. Now there is. Many corporations enjoy power of almost unbelievable scope. Conspiracy, as Dowd noted, is not necessary to the natural confluence of their interests, making their combined power enormous. Their status as multinationals increases that power still more, at the same time making control of their activities by governments problematic. Rivaling the state, and with much the same purpose as the despotic regimes of old, these corporations do not want challenges to either their interests or their power. Unlike the old despotic regimes, corporate power depends for its success not on traditional state methods of despotism, repression, and terror, but on money. This may well be a vastly more insidious kind of control.

Although the United States was founded on the ringing words of the Declaration of Independence, proclaiming that "all men are created equal," doubts about the ability of the "people" to be self-governing have been endemic in our history. Rarely disclosed by public persons, in public forums in any event, such doubts were early evidenced by Federalist policies favoring domination of government by the better educated, sounder thinkers of the "good families," mainly from the northeast. It was also present in the credo of Andrew Jackson and his followers, perhaps the most authentic champions of the rights of "the common man" to attain power produced by this nation. Yet the Jacksonian concept of "the common man" encompassed only white males. Doubts about democracy have not disappeared, and the more wealth and power one is accustomed to, the greater the doubt usually felt about leaving serious decision making to what Jacksonians called "the democracy." Yet none openly mounts a defense of autocracy, and what other alternative might there be for our representative democracy? Some form of autocracy could result from control by the few of our information distribution system.

The foregoing discussion illuminates the purpose of this book, which is to examine issues relative to the human need for information if we are democratically to make decisions. That information may include some that will appear to threaten interests of some of us, as well as some that threaten the interests of others. Because selective bites can distort, having *all* relevant information can be critically important. When do we have "all"? Unfortunately, there is no litmus test that tells us, but the more sources of information, the better the chances of access to the needed "all." The fewer outlets we have, the poorer are those chances. If we accept this premise, our future looks none too bright.

We are told that we have access through the Internet to all of the information we could possibly want. On top of that, with development of coaxial cable we will soon have more than 500 channels of "information" available from cable operators. However, with respect to the Internet, there is no easy way to search for specific information in this data morass. Is each of us so "equal" that we should be left "on our own" in the human desire to become informed? Educational institutions impose guidelines on the scope of particular disciplines. Course requirements are defined and outlined in a syllabus. If such institutions were to imitate the Internet, perhaps they should simply eliminate such guidelines, "freeing" the student to get the education she or he wants. A limited (and possibly less expensive) faculty might be on call, pulled away from research only when needed to answer student questions—if students can think of any that are sufficiently specific. Otherwise, there are the library folks, and the computer room with access to the Internet, too! Have at it, and no whimpering or whining! You don't know what it is you're supposed to be "learning"? Too bad.

As for the 500 cable channels, what if they are all owned by the same corporation, or even controlled by the same gatekeeper? How confident in such an event can anyone be of receiving "all" the information one needs? If these channels, combined with the Internet, drown a knowledge seeker in information, leaving a searching mind an addled stew, disconnect seems the only out. "Trust" has always been an important component of the transmission of information; what do we know of the source, and what level of trust can we reasonably develop in that source? Without such trust, or a mental capacity far beyond that of most, the information we get takes on the character of so many grains of sand on a beach—no reason to consider one piece or grain more important, more useful, or more correct than another.

In short, deregulation of broadcasting means freeing that medium from one of its major obligations to the public—to inform and educate. As ownership of media outlets, including those in broadcasting, becomes more concentrated in the hands of large corporations, unless there is some regulation of content by government (where else can "public" regulation come from?), broadcasters cannot be trusted to fulfill these obligations. A major purpose of this book is to urge that the inability to trust broadcasters, and the corporations controlling them, must take precedence over difficulties presented by government regulation of the medium, leaving no choice but to devise a regulatory scheme obligating broadcast licensees to take an active role in keeping the nation informed, obligations imposed by the fairness doctrine or something very much like it.

Broadcasters are not educators. They should, though, be knowledgeable about what matters are of general concern to the public at large, whether nationally or within their immediate broadcast service areas. It should also be possible to permit public input to identify issues broadcasters might not recognize. Public input could also provide a useful tool in measuring whether such coverage has been thorough and fair or requires further attention. In other words, there are ways to overcome some of the weaknesses in the fairness doctrine's role as a major, if not primary, means for keeping the electorate informed.

CHAPTER 15

The Telecommunications Act of 1996

The 1934 Communications Act was made applicable to "all interstate and foreign communication by wire or radio." The word "wire" had been added when this statute replaced the 1927 Radio Act, the scope of which was being expanded to include regulation of AT&T.[1]

AT&T owns most of the telephone lines in the United States, or did before the birth of the "Baby Bells" resulted from the consent decree that ended the government's antitrust action against Ma Bell. Whether title to those lines remains with AT&T, subject to compulsory use rights in the "Babies," or has actually been transferred to the local phone companies seems currently of little consequence for the issues covered in this book. Telephone lines have always played an important role in radio and TV. WJZ's intent to broadcast the 1922 World Series was thwarted when AT&T denied the station use of its phone lines. It remains true today that much network programming is relayed by phone lines to broadcast transmitters.

AT&T has continually flirted with involvement in aspects of telecommunications in addition to operating a telephone system. In and out of broadcasting in the first half of the 1920s, it shares with its progeny the "Baby Bells" an interest in engaging more extensively in the cable TV business than simply providing transmission lines for others. Now that traditional phone service utilizes satellites, there is no reason why such satellites should not be used to transmit all kinds of information, in competition with, or supplementary to, transmission by existing wireless and cable operations.

Computer operations also use phone lines for such services as e-mail and access to the Internet and the World Wide Web. To most of us, the world of telecommunications is enormously complex, best used with a minimum of close examination. However, all aspects of telecommunication can be reduced to the fact that the use of some form of "wire" or wireless is involved. Both of these words define FCC regulatory jurisdiction as set forth in the 1934 act. Knowingly or not, Congress placed potentially all aspects of the world of telecommunications, subject to constitutional limitations, under FCC jurisdiction, though sections in the act, as amended, place specific limitations on commission power.

Combining wire and wireless in the Communications Act also led private telecommunication players to share a common interest in watering down (if not totally ending) government regulation of their activities. Those players, increasingly limited to very large corporations, supported by theories of the Chicago school of economics, have made considerable headway, most recently in the adoption of the 1996 Telecommunications Act, in which Congress greatly reduced the areas in which the FCC would be permitted to exercise such power.

Impetus to adoption of the Telecommunications Act came from AT&T and the regional Bell companies. Restive in their roles as simply common carriers transmitting the programming of broadcasters, cable operators, and others in the information distribution business, they wanted in on the action. Broadcasters, though not the primary movers, could think of things they wanted, and if change was coming, they proposed to look to their interests.

Few members of Congress have much grasp of the intricacies of the world of telecommunications. Fewer still have either the time or the inclination to become educated about those intricacies. As we all sometimes do, they have come to rely on experts they trust to inform them. (At times we may even rely on "experts" we're not sure we trust, just because we don't want to make fools of ourselves by revealing a depth of ignorance we find embarrassing.)

Generally Congress holds hearings when considering major legislation like that designed to deregulate the telecommunications industry. Hearings in the case of the Telecommunications Act were few, and public testimony was virtually nonexistent. Instead, reliance was placed on experts. Seeing no conflict of interest, or at least none thought to be of any importance, a majority placed its trust in experts from the industry to be deregulated.

Deregulation was intended to eliminate bureaucratic bottlenecks, thus leading to a free market characterized by the flexibility needed to encourage competition and "risk taking" among the players. This in turn was intended to speed realization of the information highway and all its perceived benefits. Government and its "regulation" had been a roadblock to progress.

When you want to deal with the problems of the industry, where better to turn than the industry itself? That's what the FCC so often has done, and that's what Congress did. The Telecommunications Act was written by employees of corporations in the industry. Congress passed it. Before doing so, some congresspersons may even have read it, although anyone trying to read it now is unlikely to conclude that many congresspersons understood it.

The idea that prevailed in Congress appears to have been that the different corporations making up the industry lobby had conflicting goals because they competed with each other. Such competition is the core of the Chicago school belief in the "free market" panacea. Ergo, that competition should, it was believed, contribute to a good piece of legislation created by those most expert in the field and knowledgeable about industry problems. Although not much time has elapsed, the record so far indicates that belief was misconceived.

Reading the Telecommunications Act is an exercise in confusion, though a number of salient points important to broadcasting do emerge:[2]

1. Limitations on ownership of multiple broadcasting stations and cable outlets as well as other forms of media are significantly relaxed.

2. The stated purpose of the act is to increase competition to make the information highway a reality serving the American people at the lowest possible cost. Its intent is to create a "field wide open" to new entrants.

3. The competition to be enhanced by the act is in the entire field of telecommunications, encouraging cable operators to become telephone companies; broadcasters to become cable operators; local phone companies to become long distance carriers; and long distance carriers, competing with each other, also to enter local phone service, if they can. Because earlier legislation had barred local phone companies from competing with cable operators,[3] and the Telecommunications Act itself creates some hurdles for local phone companies attempting to enter the long distance field, it is questionable as to just how much competition Congress wanted, and where. To attribute the answer to congressional intent, though, is to perpetuate the conceit that the act was a product of the legislature, not the industry it was to benefit.

4. The term of broadcast licenses was increased to eight years from the five theretofore applicable to TV and seven for radio, and first license renewal was made virtually unchallengeable. Renewals subsequent to the

first were greatly eased by denying challengers a hearing until after the renewal question had first been decided. The act also made renewals more
difficult to challenge by implicitly reducing the importance of public service programming as a criterion for deciding the renewal question.

In legislation adopted subsequent to the 1996 act, broadcasters were
granted additional bandwidth on the spectrum to crank up for digital TV
transmission on the theory that the portion of the spectrum currently licensed could not be used for both the digital format and analog. This was
descried as a "giveaway" of public property by many, including Senators
Dole and McCain, because it effectively doubled the spectrum allotment
to each broadcast licensee. Critics advocated an auction whereby recipients
of the new bandwidth rights would have been compelled to bid for them.
Why the failure to charge for such spectrum space when no charge was
made for analog space should be so disturbing they don't explain. But,
then, the whole move to digital with its promise of technological improvements is full of vagaries and the unexplained. The world of digital TV
transmission will probably impact issues discussed in this book, but what
such impacts will be cannot now be discerned.

The Telecommunications Act intentionally leaves unanswered many
questions with respect to its provisions and usually requires the FCC to
provide those answers. Because the act in no way relieves the commission
of its normal day-to-day functions, it has resulted in a significant net increase in the commission's workload. An apparently bemused commission
issued a 48-page report enumerating, with brief description, each of the actions required to implement the act, for which Congress had appropriated
not one additional dime. Might Congress have assumed the FCC could
look to the telecommunications industry for assistance?

Shortly after the act was passed in 1996, columnist Molly Ivins commented that "one irony of the Telecommunications Act is that it was supposed to give opportunities to 'small' players. Nothing resembling small
remains in the field; we are getting stultified competition between giants"
(*Arizona Daily Star*, April 7, 1996). About 18 months later she quoted
Senator John McCain, who chairs the Senate Subcommittee on Communications, which is responsible for any possible Senate move to amend the
act: "Sadly, at least in the short run, it does not appear that the [Telecom-
munications] act is living up to the generous promises that its backers
made only two years ago. The lower rates, better service and increased
competition [have] instead been translated into high rates and increased
consolidation among big industry players." McCain has so far offered no

specifics to remedy the situation except generally to advocate further deregulation.

Ivins, one of a handful of columnists who have devoted much attention to issues raised by the Telecommunications Act, added to her comment: "As we approach the second anniversary of the Telecom Act of '96, passed by a Republican Congress at the heights of its hubris, the consequences that were (forgive me) easily foreseeable have now come to pass. The profoundly silly notion that deregulation will solve all problems—pushed for years by the free-marketeers of the Chicago school of economics—had come to be conventional wisdom among Republicans, who are, in my opinion, far too gullible about simple solutions" (*Arizona Daily Star*, January 19, 1998).

Much of the act was said to be part of a "deal" made by the corporate interests with legislative leaders, a deal some of the corporate participants are now accused of flouting. For example, SBC, Inc., is accused of going back on its word because it successfully maintained an action in a federal district court in Texas. The court threw out as unconstitutional restrictions in the carefully crafted law to which SBC allegedly had agreed, restrictions making it difficult, perhaps impossible, for SBC (and other "Baby Bells") to enter the long distance phone market. Earlier the 8th Circuit Federal Court of Appeals, in a case representing interests of local phone service carriers, invalidated complex rules devised by the FCC dealing with local phone rates (*Iowa Public Utilities Board v. FCC* 120 F.3d 753, 1997). The rules were designed to implement procompetition objectives by removing obstacles to entry into local markets by long distance carriers. Their adoption was said by the court to be in excess of the FCC's power under the act. Specifics of the rules involved are not as important as that the court's treatment of the Telecommunications Act indicates how difficult it is to make sense of its alleged objective of furthering competition in order to implement it. Considering motives of the corporate authors as they drafted the Telecommunications Act, one is reminded of Congressman Lionel Van Deerlin's observation when his attempted rewrite of the Communications Act failed. "All [the broadcasters' representatives] want for their clients," he said, "is 'a fair advantage.'" Recently some wag paraphrased this statement to declare that all they want is an "unfair advantage." That people so motivated might produce a legislative mishmash is not surprising.

Two recent matters shed light on our futures under the Telecom Act. AT&T made a successful bid to purchase the nation's largest TV cable company, MediaOne Group. The acquisition, still to be okayed by the FTC, drew criticism because of its obvious monopolistic possibilities. Responding to such criticisms, AT&T's chairman, C. Michael Armstrong, is quoted as saying, "The more you buy from AT&T, the less it's going to cost you." One wonders if Mr. Armstrong had any clear idea of the implications of what he said.

The second matter is more complicated. The Telecom Act requires regional phone companies to negotiate with those wishing to use their physical facilities, like phone lines on poles, for reasonable use fees to provide competitive local phone service. It further requires that regional Bells propose a reasonable fee for use of the Bell's physical facilities by competitors in providing local phone service in competition with the Bell company. U.S. West, a regional Bell in the Southwest, arrived at a figure of $22 per customer per month for use of its facilities in Arizona. AT&T complained that this was too much; the charge should have been $16. Hold on–what has AT&T to do with this? If U.S. West complies with the statutory requirement to propose such a fee, it is then free to provide long distance service in Arizona in competition with AT&T. Thus AT&T, joined by MCI and other long distance providers, share a common interest in keeping U.S. West out of the long distance market. Existing long distance servers aside, others have also contended the U.S. West rate is too high. Who decides? The FCC, apparently acting within its delegated authority under the Telecom Act, claims it has the authority, but the Arizona Public Utilities Commission claims *it* does, saying it's a matter of "states' rights." In vindication of such "rights," it approved the $22 rate, and a federal district court upheld that rate (though not necessarily the "right"), apparently believing the Bell company had complied with the law regardless of whether final authority belonged to the FCC or the state Public Utilities Commission. Paraphrasing Molly Ivins, no pygmies are involved in these disputes. Giants are vying for control of as much of the pie as they can get, and remember, the more you buy from AT&T, the less it's going to cost you.

Belief that corporations that control our information distribution system are dedicated to keeping the American people informed is, to put it gently, questionable. Each of them is certainly interested in garnering as big a piece of that system as it can. The Telecom Act is complex, and the stakes for the giant players are enormous. Courts, already drafted to resolve some of the statute's ambiguities, will play an ever-increasing role. AT&T has already filed suit to challenge the U.S. West user fee rate for local phone competition.

People have consciences; people can be said to have ethical obligations. Corporations are not "people," notwithstanding the judicial fiction.

They have no consciences. They are obliged to no one but their share-holders—and that obligation is to maximize the return on shareholder investment. Persons in corporate management can either assume such obligations on the part of their employer or quit. A preeminent spokesman for understanding the nature of the obligations of corporate management, Milton Friedman, has pointed out that claims that such persons have a "social responsibility" undermines the entire meaning of capitalism in a free society. The obligation of management, he emphasizes, is to the corporation's owners, its shareholders; the obligation is fulfilled by making as much money for such shareholders as possible (Friedman 1962, 133). Courts have taken a like view. See, for example, *Dodge v. Ford Motor Co.* 204 Mich. 459 (1919). To talk about being "disappointed" with a corporation because of actions taken by corporate managers *for the corporation* is foolish, if understandable in light of our inability to find a means for legal distinction between real people and these single-purpose legal fictions called "corporations."

When the *Arizona Daily Star* (May 11, 1999) reported on the $22 U.S. West fee and AT&T's opposition to it, the item was described in the paper's contents section on page 2 as, "A federal judge disappoints consumer groups clamoring for competition in local telephone service."

Unlikely as one might have been even to suspect the existence of such consumer groups, reading about them might hearten the reader until, turning to the story itself, one learns that these groups have something in common with "spontaneous" Baghdad demonstrators in support of Saddam Hussein. The article tells us that these consumer groups were brought together for a press conference by Arizonans for Competition in Telephone Service, "[an] organization funded largely by AT&T, MCI, and other long distance carriers that want to keep U.S. West out of the [long distance] business" (*Arizona Daily Star,* part B).

Many free marketers believe the free market, unburdened of government regulation, can solve all problems. If steps in that direction fail of their objective, the market obviously is not completely free, a conclusion greatly to the advantage of the devout free marketers. They can never be proved wrong.

In fact, markets are never completely free of regulation. Market participants themselves constantly seek legislative advantages. Not all the money they pour into lobbying is for the purpose of preventing government encroachment into their domains. As employees of media corporations, and human to boot, most journalists are unwilling to risk either life or livelihood in service of some "public right to know." Reportorial dedication is not enough to produce such motivation; such service requires a work environment that encourages it. Corporate America, operating in the "free market," does not provide such an environment. Because we cannot place our reliance on operation of the free market to perform broadcasting's information-providing role, and broadcasting is not staffed with professional educators, citizens can only look to themselves. Effective citizen action, though, requires assistance from the chief representative of the citizenry, their government.

There may be alternative means to some form of fairness doctrine to produce in broadcast programming the sort of broadcaster/listener interplay the free market is said to produce but doesn't. There may be other ways the electronic media may be motivated to perform the educational role here ascribed to it. The fairness doctrine, though, has one advantage over possible alternatives in having been fleshed out through years of operation. It did produce coverage of some controversial issues even if its operation was not perfect.

To study the complexities involved in this dynamic field of telecommunications and other media by which Americans are kept informed, Dean Lee Bollinger of the University of Michigan Law School suggested appointment of a new commission like the Hutchins Commission, which undertook a study of the media in 1943. Professor Robert McChesney sees, I think accurately, a wide-ranging threat to our democratic system, including media control, in the sort of explosive growth of corporate power and wealth I have alluded to. He has urged vast segments of our society to rise in a coordinated defense of popular sovereignty (McChesney 1997, 66). Worthwhile as both approaches are, each faces difficulty in even getting started. I would add to these two that Congress reenact the fairness doctrine. Such a step would not be easily achieved; in fact, it is unlikely to occur in the legislative climate currently prevailing. But reenactment down the road is not impossible, particularly if electoral support for such restoration is stimulated. Return of the fairness doctrine would not be a substitute for the other two approaches, but it might well be the easiest of the three to achieve.

Reintroduction of the doctrine just might make a substantial contribution to fostering the complete coverage of relevant issues that is needed to enable a free people to make intelligent decisions. In addition to the fact that we have had experience with use of the doctrine, it also withstood constitutional attack in the *Red Lion* case. Its inability to define a controversial issue could be made less important by inviting a public contribution to its "meaning." Broadcast licensees could be required to make periodic announcements of their obligations under the doctrine and invite listeners' suggestions about "controversial issues" that should be covered. Use of the doctrine might also improve if the independence of FCC commissioners was strengthened vis-à-vis individual members of Congress, by lengthening commissioner terms. Commissioners could also be freed from some undesirable industry pressure by barring them from accepting employment within the regulated sector for at least five years after leaving the FCC.

If the doctrine worked as hoped, it might also energize nonbroadcast reporters to exercise more journalistic courage. Speech "rights" of corporations might be compromised; those of their journalistic employees—as well as of the public—enhanced. The alternative to some government intervention in program content is to leave complete control of such programming in the pretty much noncompetitive world of large corporations, whose aim is to cause each and all to look to fewer and fewer of them for more and more of our needs. Hey, the more you look to us, the less it'll cost you!

Just as this story began with the creation of RCA, that corporation's end sheds light on our position today. When David Sarnoff died, his son took over as RCA's president. Unlike the sins of the fathers, the skills of the fathers possibly are not visited unto even the second generation. In any case, following Sarnoff senior's death, RCA's fortunes went into decline. In 1986 GE, which had created RCA in 1919, absorbed it and proceeded to dismember it, selling off those parts that it had no interest in retaining. What it wanted, it kept—including the National Broadcasting Company—which it owns to this day.

Of GE's ownership of NBC and its effect on broadcasting, Martin A. Lee, publisher of *Extra!* the journal of FAIR (Fairness & Accuracy in Reporting), the New York–based media watch group, wrote:

> The National Broadcasting Corporation (NBC), one of the three leading U.S. commercial television networks, is owned by GE, a major military contractor. As it turned out, GE designed, manufactured or supplied parts or maintenance for nearly every important weapons system employed by the USA during the Gulf War, including the much-praised Patriot and Tomahawk Cruise missiles, the Stealth bomber, the B-52 bomber, the AWACS plane, the Apache and Cobra helicopters and the NAVSTAR spy satellite system.
>
> Few TV viewers . . . were aware of the inherent conflict of interest

whenever NBC correspondents and consultants hailed the performance of U.S. weapons. In nearly every instance they were extolling equipment made by GE, the corporation that pays their salaries. . . .

A former NBC News employee underscored the dilemma: "The whole notion of freedom of the press becomes a contradiction when the people who own the media are the same people who need to be reported on." (Lee 1991, 29)

Perhaps the fairness doctrine would compromise NBC's "speech" rights, and thus those of GE. Perhaps, though, restoration of the doctrine is the best means at hand with a reasonable chance to protect the *public's* First Amendment rights, at least within the electronic media—rights that are so important to a democratic society and so threatened by, among other concentrations of media power, GE's ownership of NBC.

Notes

1. It was the word "wire" that operated to sweep CATV into the FCC's regulatory net in 1968.

2. Professor Patricia Aufderheide (1999) has provided the first attempt at comprehensive analysis of the Telecommunications Act.

3. This provision was held unconstitutional in *Chesapeake and Potomac Telephone Co. of Virginia v. U.S.* 42 F.3d 181 (4th Cir., 1994), a decision the Supreme Court had agreed to review. Undoubtedly because of the change wrought in the Telecommunications Act, the high court returned the case to the lower court for determination as to whether the issues had become moot.

Conclusion

I n *The Ends of the Earth*, Robert Kaplan tells of a conversation with a former government minister of Sierra Leone about magic and the part it plays in conditions of instability in West Africa. The former minister told about a young woman who assisted rebel forces by burying magic charms behind enemy lines. She would then "make herself invisible" by walking backward, naked, looking over her shoulder into a mirror to find her way.

After a pause the minister pointed to an old transistor on the table, saying, "[But] the greatest magic is the radio. This box, it talks to you, in your own language. Yet it has no wires connecting it to anything. Now, that's magic! Therefore, whatever comes out of this box must be true. This box is how Sekou Toure ruled Guinea for so long. . . . the radio—a way to control a population through magic" (Kaplan 1996, 33-34).

A subtle and complex form of "magic" indeed.

We in the United States are not bedeviled with beliefs that the talking box, even when accompanied by pictures, is magic. Sometimes we may even question the truth of what we are told, though a great majority of us acknowledge this kind of box to be the major source of our information about the world.

In the Supreme Court's decision in *FCC v. Pottsville Broadcasting* 309 U.S. 134, 137 (1939), Justice Frankfurter wrote that government control of the broadcasting spectrum was motivated by concern that the medium would otherwise be "subordinated to monopolistic domination." Such concern was voiced by the primary author of both the Radio and the Communications acts, Clarence Dill of Washington (see 319 U.S. 190, 221, note 5) and has been mentioned by both commission and courts on many occasions. They have not, though, provided the Communications Commission with any consistent direction. Seeming to ignore underlying questions of "control," some commissioners emphasized concern over use of broadcasting for purely private gain, subverting the requirement to serve the public interest, whereas others saw the more serious threat as being *to* broadcasters' rights. Stressing free speech rights of licensees, these commissioners were more inclined than other commissioners to place their trust in the operation of a free, competitive market. The commissions have vacillated between these two positions, sometimes exercising more, sometimes less, influence over program content; sometimes imposing more, then relaxing and substituting less, control over the extent of audience reach that could be controlled by a single broadcasting interest. The most consistently applied policy was one of inconsistency.

In the last thirty years the trend has clearly been favorable to broadcasters. It has afforded them greater freedom to act as they wish and program what they wish, without official intrusion. An exception has been material deemed morally offensive from a sexual point of view, but that concern has had a limited reach, and one of doubtful effectiveness.

As concern for any sort of government role in determining the nature of the "public interest" that broadcasting is to serve has diminished (for so the Communications Act still provides, even though the meaning of those words has become more problematic) so has concern for diversity of broadcasting sources. So also has concern about monopolization of the airwaves, prevention of which Justice Frankfurter saw as a prime motive for government regulation in the first place. Monopolization is evidenced by the uniformity of views expressed in most programming, regardless of ownership of a particular station. This is partly due to broadcasting's role as servant— not of the public and its interest, but of the advertiser and his or her interest, and the perception of a certain beauty in the subtle blend of advertising matter with program content, initially noted by NBC's first president, Merlin Aylesworth, in the early days of broadcasting.

Today monopolization has become even more overt as the size of the total listening audience that may fall under the broadcasting sway of any one ownership interest has expanded. That is what the Telecommunications Act is giving us and, in doing so, has created a brotherhood characterized by great wealth, by managements accountable only to shareholders, and shareholders who number in the tens of thousands—rendering any effective shareholder control over management unrealistic. It is this system that is the source of the entertainment—and the news, the *news*—we receive over "the box." As government power to regulate programming fades, a small group of individuals, sharing common values, accountable to no one but themselves, fills the vacuum in the name of "freedom." We would do well to remember the power of the box, and what the government minister in Sierra Leone told Robert Kaplan concerning its magical ability to perpetuate "rule." We would do well to remember views expressed by George Orwell in *1984*, even as he may have misconceived the source of the threat.

Solutions do not easily come to mind. I have suggested one: restoration of the fairness doctrine, one goal for which this book was written. It is a specific and concrete step, involving minimal government intrusion, but a step that would be stoutly resisted by broadcasters. Proposed restoration would be met with cries of anguish and warnings against "trampling on First Amendment rights"—cries that ignore such rights in listeners. The charge would be led by powerful corporations, backed by their articulate academic defenders. Such forces could be overcome only with the help of a motivated public, assuring its government that it conceives service of the public interest to be a major obligation of broadcasters, and a rather minor charge for the valuable rights they enjoy: something like what was intended by the Communications Act in the first place.

References

Aufderheide, Patricia. 1999. *Communications Policy and the Public Interest*. New York and London: Guilford Press.

Bagdikian, Ben. 1994. *Media Monopoly*. 4th ed. Boston: Beacon Press.

Barendt, Eric. 1993. *Broadcasting Law*. New York: Oxford University Press.

Bergreen, Laurence. 1980. *Look Now, Pay Later: The Rise of Network Broadcasting*. Garden City, N.Y.: Doubleday.

Bollinger, Lee C. 1993. *Images of a Free Press*. Chicago and London: University of Chicago Press.

Caro, Robert A. 1990. *The Years of Lyndon Johnson*. Vol. 2. New York: Alfred A Knopf.

Carter, T. Barton, et al. 1994. *Mass Communication Law in a Nutshell*. 4th ed. St. Paul, Minn.: West Publishing.

Case, Josephine, and Everett Case. 1982. *Owen D. Young and American Enterprise*: Boston, Mass.: David R. Gordine.

Coase, Ronald A. 1959. "The Federal Communications Commission." *Journal of Law and Economics* 2:1.

————. 1965. "Evaluation of Public Policy Relating to Radio and Television Broadcasting: Social and Economic Issues." *Land Economics* 41:161.

Congressional Record. 1912. 62nd Cong., 2nd sess., 7574.

Dallek, Robert. 1991. *Lone Star Rising, Lyndon Johnson and His Times 1908-1960*. New York: Oxford University Press.

De Vany, Arthur S., et al. 1980. *A Property System Approach to the Electromagnetic Spectrum:* San Francisco, Calif.: Cato Institute.

Douglas, Susan J. 1987. *Inventing American Broadcasting, 1899–1922*, Baltimore, Md.: Johns Hopkins University Press.

Dowd, Douglas. 1997. *Against the Conventional Wisdom*. Boulder, Colo.: Westview Press.

Dreher, Carl. 1977. *Sarnoff: An American Success*. New York: Quadrangle/*New York Times*.

Emery, Walter B. 1971. *Broadcasting and Government: Responsibilities and Regulation*. East Lansing: Michigan State University Press.

First Annual Federal Radio Commission Report to Congress, 1928. 1971. In *History of Broadcasting: Radio to Television*. New York: Arno Press/*New York Times*.

Friedman, Milton. 1962. *Capitalism and Freedom*. Chicago: University of Chicago Press.

Hayek, Friedrich A. 1944. *The Road to Serfdom:* Chicago: University of Chicago Press.

Hilliard, Robert L. 1991. *The Federal Communications Commission: A Primer.* Boston, Mass.: Focal Press.

Jung, Donald J. 1996. *The Federal Communications Commission, the Broadcast Industry, and the Fairness Doctrine, 1981–1987.* Lanham, Md.: University Press of America.

Kahn, Frank J., ed. 1978. *Documents of American Broadcasting.* 3d ed. New York: Prentice Hall.

Kalven, Harry. 1967. "Broadcasting, Public Policy, and the First Amendment." *Journal of Law and Economics* 10:15.

Kaplan, Robert. 1996. *The Ends of the Earth.* New York: Vintage Books.

Krattenmaker, Thomas G., and Lucas A. Powe Jr. 1994. *Regulating Broadcast Programming.* Cambridge, Mass.: MIT Press/AEI Press.

Lee, Martin A. 1991. "Arms and the Media: Business as Usual." *Index on Censorship* 10 (1991): 29.

Lewis, Tom. 1991. *Empire of the Air: The Men Who Made Radio.* New York: Edward Burlingame Books.

McChesney, Robert W. 1993. *Telecommunications, Mass Media, and Democracy: The Battle for Control of University Broadcasting, 1928–1935.* New York: Oxford University Press.

————. 1997. *Corporate Media and the Threat to Democracy.* New York: Seven Stories Press.

Minow, Newton, and Craig L. LaMay. 1995. *Abandoned in the Wasteland.* New York: Hill and Wang.

Powe, Lucas A. Jr. 1987. *American Broadcasting and the First Amendment.* Berkeley: University of California Press.

Proceedings of the Fourth National Radio Conference and Recommendations for Regulation of Radio. 1925. Washington, D.C.: Government Printing Office, 1926.

Sobel, Robert, 1986. *RCA.* New York: Stein and Day.

U.S. Department of Commerce. 1922. *Minutes of Conference on Radio Telephony.* Washington, D.C., February 27 and 28.

Ventura Free Press. 1932. *The Empire of the Air.* Ventura, Calif.: H. O. Davis.

Weinberg, Steve. 1983. "The Politics of Rewriting the Federal Communications Act." In *Communications Policy and the Political Process,* ed. John J. Havick. Westport, Conn: Greenwood Press.

Wyman, Bruce. 1906. *Cases on Public Service Companies.* Cambridge, Mass.: Harvard University Press.

Index

ISBN 0-8138-2568-7